Everyone Has a Story to Tell

Everyone Has a Story to Tell

BY

Evans High School BETA Club

Foreword by
Jennifer Bohn

Published by
Bookstand Publishing
Gilroy, CA 95020
2100_6

Copyright © 2007 by Evans High School
And Jennifer Bohn
All rights reserved. No part of this publication may be reproduced or transmitted in any form or by any means, electronic or mechanical, including photocopy, recording, or any information storage and retrieval system, without permission in writing from the copyright owner.

978-1-58909-423-9

Printed in the United States of America

Acknowledgements

The following organizations and individuals have made a meaningful contribution to the success of this project! ***Thank you!***

University of Florida College of Education
Count Me In! Grant Orange County Foundations
OCPS Mini-Service Learning Grant
Orlando Coalition for the Homeless
Dr. Wanda Lastrapes
Anthony Martin
Charlie Grace
Crystal Scott
Marie Shafranski
Jennifer Sheredy
Keith Miller
Mary Chair
Tracy Michalski
Kenya Nelson-Warren
Ray Bornacelli
Sandy Irizarry
Frank and Sandy Engle
Roy and Deb Haggerty
Kathleen Shaffer
Jeff and Gaye Clark

Foreword by: Jennifer Bohn

 This project was born from love. I remain in gratitude to my mom who has been my greatest example of living love and to the students at Evans High School who have made me a better teacher and a better human being.

 It has been an honor to teach at Maynard Evans High School for the past twelve years. It is a result of working with the most incredible young people in the world that such motivation and inspiration in me exists. Daily I find myself in awe of our youth. In the eyes of the Florida Department of Education, Evans High School is failing....a school in crisis. Although this conclusion has been based on poor performance on the FCAT- a state mandated test, the failure that really occurs can be found in the epidemic of poverty... poverty that fuels the day to day struggle that directly impacts children. I am witness to the wave of teen pregnancy, the drastic increase in teen on teen crime and violence, the intolerance of other cultures... seeing pride as a wall or barrier, as opposed to a bridge and a celebration, the lack of resources, and parents whose knowledge base is limited and whose involvement in the school partnership has been almost non-existent. As a result, academic excellence is in jeopardy.

What I know for sure is our children want better. Due to the financial struggles, I know many of our students and their families are on the brink of homelessness. I have listened to the heartbreaking stories, time after time, of students going home to no power. I have assisted my students' families with paying rent to avoid eviction and I have tracked the house hopping of many students as they have been shuffled between extended families and family friends for shelter. I have taught students who have lived in hotels and have had to wake up two hours earlier than most to ride public transportation across town to get to school. Solutions exist: strengthening leadership skills, maximizing resources, and developing community motivation.

Awareness of homelessness is imperative. Preserving humanity from poverty is critical. In the past year there has been a rash of homeless beatings by teenagers. In the end, we must remain human. We must encourage tolerance. We must instill hope in others. We must have no other choice than to elevate each other because in turn, we elevate ourselves. **Now** is the time for us to act. **Now** exists an opportunity to get involved in a meaningful, and deeply challenging endeavor to put a "face" to those we often walk by in disgust, those to whom we turn our heads at or put our noses up to because...."**Everyone** Has a Story to Tell."

Table of Contents

"Hello Is Easy"... 1

"The Lady's Man".. 4

"Not Every Homeless Person Is On Drugs"....................... 9

"A Life For My Children"... 13

"His Name Is…".. 15

"Stay In School".. 21

"Unpredictable Saturday"... 26

"Treat Others As You Would Like to Be Treated"........... 30

"Can You Really Tell?"... 33

"God Has A Plan for All of Us"..................................... 37

"The Untouchable".. 40

"Mr. Bob".. 44

"It's Easy To Do Wrong".. 48

"Linnie Johnson"... 53

"Kelvina".. 56

"The Dream Of A Woman Filled With Hope"................. 59

"Frank D. Crosby"... 62

"Momma's Always There".. 69

"Daughter Of The Homeless"....................................... 77

"Lasted"……………………………………………..……..79

"A Regular Life" 80

"Miguel"... …83

"The Life of a Homeless Man"…………………....……..86

"A Better Path" 90

"Females Are Better" 92
"Control Your Destiny" 95
"What Causes Me To Be Homeless Is Bad Luck" 102
"Nothing Worth Achieving Is Easy" 104
"Dear Diary" 108
"A Normal Life" 111
Reflections 120-138

"Hello Is Easy"
By Khadija McPhee

Every time I go to work, this very strange homeless man says hello to me. He is always pushing an old bike with rags hanging and plastic bags fanning from the handle bars. Everyday I fearfully return his greeting and he smiles. But one day I ignored my fear of him and I asked, "Why do you always speak to me and smile?" He smiled at my question and suddenly his expression turned grave. He looked down at his bike and in a low voice brimmed with sorrow, anger, and bewilderment, "Of all these people that walk 'round dis here plaza, you the only one that ever says anything back to me."

I stood there dumbfounded, a slew of emotions surged through my veins. I wanted to say something, but before I could say anything to him he smiled, nodded his head, and walked away. He continued to depart as I dramatically searched for something, anything to say, but my brain and vocal cords would not coincide. He vanished around the corner and although my mind was screaming, "run, go after him," my legs would not move; he was gone.

Abandoned, robbed, beaten, raped, and addicted; imagine that life. Being disowned by your loved ones, robbed by strangers, beaten by friends, and raped by family, realizing that your only friend in life is a vial filled with death and a syringe analogous to suicide. In this big world we call home, filled with family, friends and dreams, all around you is happiness. All around you is love, but the only things that you can grasp are despair, longing, and misery. Imagine a world so big with thousands of possibilities and yet none of the positive ones ever cross your path. If life was a game of poker, everyone seemed to have four-of-a-kind except you. You were dealt the worse hand of the game. Imagine a face to this life, an elderly African-American man with full lips, almond-shaped eyes, graying hair, and a heart of gold; a man who lives, breathes, thinks, and feels; a man who had hopes and dreams and aspirations. To this man, this imaginary life isn't imaginary at all. It's the reality that he must face everyday.

With simple observations of a person, one can only see the surface details, but through deep thought and conversation a person can truly understand a man. To everyone walking by on the street he seems to be just another broken part of humanity; that part of society we don't want to see… unworthy of even the simplest 'hello.' But if someone would have taken the time to converse with this man, those shallow first impressions would have been instantaneously shattered. How many of us have the courage to step out of our safety zone and say *hello*?

"The Lady's Man"
By Candice Haughton and Tamillya Arnett

When we first saw Mark, he was lying on the floor that he dubbed his bed, reading the Bible. He seemed to be looking for something, anything that would take him out of the world of misery, drugs, confusion, and loneliness that he called his life. He hoped that maybe he would find an answer that could change everything. It had occurred to me that he was going through a lot because many people who seek God, especially those who are in serious situations, are so desperate that they have to rely on faith in someone or something they can't even see.

Mark grew up in the slums of Washington D.C. with both of his parents and five brothers and sisters. Unfortunately, both of his parents were alcoholics. Despite their problems the family seemed to be quite close. While his father worked as a gas pump attendant, his mother stayed home to take care of the children. As a young child Mark recalls his mother taking him to his cousin's house to play on weekends.

During his elementary, middle, and high school years, the majority was actually the minority. The student body was composed mostly of African Americans and Hispanics. He spoke with great pride when he explained how popular he was not only in his school, but in his entire community. His smile grew even wider when he spoke about the many girls he was involved with and how he was known as "the lady's man." He laughed as he sophomorically recalled his relationships, how they began and how they ended.

When I asked him about his fondest memory of high school, a look of euphoria immediately enchanted his eyes; his eyes had a glow that wasn't there before. Without hesitation he recalled his high school choir and how much of an impact it made on his life. He was so excited that he went on to tell me how he sang a solo on a Christmas special called "Christmas in Washington" and how his choir even sang for former President George Bush, Sr. once before. When I asked him what he decided to do after high school, a look of hopelessness recaptured his eyes.

After high school he explained with great nostalgia how he painfully ended three relationships with women he was formerly engaged to. After three failed attempts to marry, he dropped out of college during his freshman year and moved from job to job. To name a few, he was a carpet layer, cashier, short-order cook, and electrical worker.

Eventually he became chronically depressed and had to move in with his sister for support because of his inability to keep a job.

It was at this time, he explained, that he decided to turn to drugs in order to ease the troubles that he faced in his life. As he continued to share with us his experiences with drugs, his eyes began to dilate, as if he were going through another high. He then went on to describe a flashback of himself speaking to a doll which was not only a hallucination due to the drugs that he was taking, but also a part of his psychotic condition. "The doll called my name and said that I would die, over and over again," Mark said with a bit of trepidation, pacified by an uneasy and forced chuckle. As if he had a split personality, his mood suddenly changed from disconnected to positive.

As we listened to him carry on about his struggle with drugs, it slowly evolved into a discussion about his past and current mental state. He talked about being admitted into different mental institutions by his sister during the period between leaving college and moving in with her. He described how we would sometimes walk from one state to another. "By the time I had walked about ten miles, my feet felt as if they were on fire, like the ground was made of hot coals and every time I took another step, my feet grew hotter and hotter."

He went into detail about his illness. "I remember waking up in my bed at the house and just laughing at the jokes my cousins and friends told me in my head, and I would go on throughout the day like this just laughing." He finally decided that he wanted to run away and make a life of his own, a life outside of the "mad house." Whenever we asked him how he managed to leave the mental hospital, he would evade the question and make a joke about something that happened at the Coalition.

As our conversation came to a close, Mark told us that he felt that his life was over because of all of the dumb mistakes he made throughout his life and because he had his priorities mixed up. He even went on to encourage us to be the best people that we can be. It was at that moment that we felt a connection with Mark. For an instant we felt what he felt, the sorrow and the pain that he went through in his life. It brought tears to our eyes. Mark told us not to worry about him. He said that it felt good to simply share his story to someone who actually wanted to listen. We parted with mutual smiles as if we understood something new about each other, even though everything that was learned came from his mouth, experiences, and his heart.

"Not Every Homeless Person Is On Drugs"
By Jessica Laracuente and Almendra Vegas

Eager and willing to share her story, Danielle greeted us with a smile. As we sat down she immediately wanted to get started. "Not every homeless person is on drugs or has co-dependency; they are just normal people trying to make it in life."

You see, Danielle wanted to make it perfectly clear that not all stereotypes of homeless people are true. She was only homeless because of a simple move she and her family decided to make to Florida. When Danielle and her family moved to Florida they found themselves in a financial battle. A move she thought would change her life for good took a sad turn, leaving her homeless.

Danielle was born near Chicago in Oak Park, Illinois, a place she believes contains her fondest memories of her father. She later moved to Mississippi where she was raised by her mother. When asked about her mother she slumped down, chuckled softly and asked, "You want the truth?" She then went on to describe her mother as honestly as she could using only two words that wouldn't offend her mother's memory. Those two words were simply, "fuss-box." As we sat there looking at her we couldn't help but think how incredible it was for someone in her position to feel the need to protect her mother's memory even though she was never really there for Danielle.

As a child her life was no different from anyone else's. Like most children she was very shy and didn't like school very much due to being teased and bullied by others. Despite her shyness, her dream was to become a singer like her role model Whitney Houston. As an adult she got married, pregnant, and started a family of her own. Danielle's four kids were sitting next to us, chattering to each other. These weren't kids stricken with the sadness of being homeless. We thought in astonishment, how could these little children, barely 6 years old, smile considering their situation? In order to provide for herself, Danielle had a vast myriad of jobs, ranging from telemarketing to customer service.

Over the years she gradually began losing touch with several of her relatives, only remaining in contact with a few of them. When asked what her happiest moment in life was, she replied without hesitation, "When I got my first apartment and completed trade school." However, those happy moments were soon overshadowed by several struggles, including trying to keep her marriage together and going back to school to get her life back on track. Even with her struggles in life, Danielle never went down the path of drugs and crime. In fact, the only thing she is really guilty of is getting a speeding ticket, which explains why she has no regrets in life. She's been homeless for about three months now and the only thing she really worries about are her children's futures.

Danielle, like every other average person in the world, gets about eight hours of sleep each day. She then wakes up to prepare her kids for another day at school and puts them safely on the bus. In an attempt to get a fresh start in life she then heads off to Mid-Florida Tech where she takes classes until five in the afternoon. After a long day of studying and hard thinking, she returns home to prepare a meal for her family, puts the kids off to bed, and gets ready to repeat the process the next day.

Being homeless doesn't stop Danielle from dreaming big. Her current goals are to continue furthering her education, save money, and start a real estate business of her own. Hopefully someday this will give her the chance to live the life of her dreams, which consists of owning her own house, car, pets, and having a normal marriage. As our interview came to a close Danielle left us with one final statement: "Don't ever stay with a guy who hits you, leave him."

"A Life for My Children"
By Jose Vazquez

My name is Suzanne and I am forty-three years old. I have two boys ages six months and ten years. I have been homeless since January, 2006. I was born in the Bronx, NY. The thing I remember the most about my childhood is that in the Bronx, there were a lot of different faces and everyone was always in a hurry to get somewhere.

I remember that my parents were always positive and they always helped me; right now they are in Heaven. I still keep in contact with some of my family in New York City. My dreams have always been to travel and to settle down and to get the goodness out of life. My childhood was a good one; I was in the Girl Scouts and when I was fourteen I had a job so I could have money in my pocket instead of asking my parents.

I say that schools here in Florida are further behind schools in New York because in Florida a lot of students just want to get by or get a GED, while in New York people want to pursue their education. While growing up I worked in supermarkets and department stores. I also had a job in a telephone company. All the money I earned I saved so I could travel.

My happiest moments in life were when I went on vacations because I never had to worry about anything. I loved to get different kinds of perfume and go dancing on Friday nights. The biggest challenge I have had is being homeless, but I will always think of it as a minor setback.

A regular day for me is getting my kid ready for school, taking my other child to daycare, and then going to find job opportunities. The main reason I became homeless is that I have to support two kids with jobs that don't pay enough. Not many people mistreat me; I get treated just like everyone else. I treat others the same way I want to be treated.

If I could change anything about Florida it would be that a high school diploma is mandatory; no GED's. Everything I do, I do it for my children. I try to give them a better life. My advice for everyone who is going to read this is that you should cherish what you have because you never know when it can be taken from you.

"His Name Is…"

By Stephanie Cineas and Thien An Pham

Imagine yourself walking and you see a man. He is sitting down twisting his hair. You can see he is in the process of growing dreads. His hair is messy and looks as if it has not been combed in a while. His hair looks unclean and sticks outs in dry clumps. You think his hair has an odor because it looks so dirty. Your fingers begin to itch and a feeling of wanting to comb his hair starts to overcome you. The first word that comes to mind is "bum." It is hard to look past his hair and see his face. But once you get past the hair, you see the face of a man who is homeless but trying to put his life together. You can see his pain, loneliness, the hurt of being unwanted, and regret. His name is Damien.

Everyone regrets something; some may regret not listening to their parents, not hanging out with the right friends, or not taking education seriously. What regrets would a homeless person have? You would think they would regret being born into a family that does not want them, and regret dropping out of school, but not Damien. Of all the experiences Damien has gone through in his life, he only regrets one thing: "I should've let my daddy cut my hair when I was a baby. I probably would be a different person."

When we asked Damien what he meant when he said he would be a different person, he responded, "I probably wouldn't be homeless." But who would have known he would be homeless and living at a homeless shelter?

Damien Javon Hill was born on April 27, 1986 in Greenville, Alaska. Being that both his mother and father were Muslims, Damien grew up in this culture. "I remember they only spoke Arabian." Judging by the sparkle in his eye and the smile of his face, it's quite obvious Damien loves his family. He remembers his father's *blessed meals*; "my dad was a preacher and a chef. He used to make dinners and drive around selling them."

Damien lived a "normal" childhood. At age 17, he started moving around and lived in Georgia, Alabama, and Florida. "I remember I used to hang out with older kids. The kids my age liked to start stuff. They used to always try to get into a fight. I used to hang with them, but when they got into a fight, I didn't have their back; they fought over stupid things."

Like any teenage boy, Damien loved to play football. With an extra bit of pride, Damien told us how he played at Glen Middle School and at the Job Corps in Bronxville, Georgia. Although he enjoyed school, Damien decided to drop out in the eleventh grade. Looking back, Damien says school "is a good thing." Looking in our eyes, Damien encouraged us to "concentrate" and take things "one step at a time."

"I wanted to be a bodybuilder" was his answer when I asked him what his childhood dreams were; "A bodybuilder or a model." Damien remembers his stepmother telling him he should be a model because he was good-looking. When he dropped out of school, Damien became a salesman. He worked at his brother's barbershop where he sold CDs, DVDs, shoes, purses, and modeled clothes. I'm guessing, as a result of working for his brother, Damien's dream began to percolate.

Now, he wants to open his own shop and do what he is happy doing and is good at. As he was telling us his dreams, we could see he was determined. His tone changed from being reserved to confident and unstoppable. We thought this was just some silly notion, but when we asked how he was going to achieve his goals, it was evident he had it all planned out. "I gotta get the number to get the clothes from my brother in Georgia, start at a shop to learn the business, get the DVDs, CDs, and purses, get a license, buy a computer, open a checking account" and the to-do list went on. He even has a media campaign in which he would model his clothes and have commercials that advertised when and where his products would be sold. When we asked if he would need any support or help, he sat back, with no doubt in his voice he replied "Naw, I'ma do this on my own."

If he would have told us this in the beginning, we would have thought it was fabricated. But Damien really is working at this dream of his. He has two jobs; in the morning he works at the Liverpool and in the evening at Kress Choppa House. Damien informed us of a little known fact; "homeless people have the chance to become rich because of having no bills." He told us that the homeless shelter has places where you can put a deposit down for ninety-nine dollars a week.

As Damien was telling us his story, we wondered how he became homeless. He says the reason he is homeless is because of his stepmother. At age 17, his stepmother no longer wanted to shelter him and persuaded his father to put him out. Although most people, including myself, would have a grudge against their parents, Damien does not. "They have their own life and think I should have my own" was how he reasoned them putting him out. We asked him how he felt about being homeless, and he said he does not feel ready to be on his own.

When talking about his family, Damien's body language changed. We could see his eyes were watery; he became soft-spoken, and somewhat reserved. Looking at him, we could imagine that he felt alone and unwanted. At times, he would start to say something, but would then stop, and start a new sentence.

Damien stays in contact with his family. He has a grandma in Daytona which he sometimes visits, and he calls his other family members. Some nights, when his brother is in town, Damien spends the night at his brother's house on Kaley Street. Although his brother treats him well, when his friends are around his brother changes towards him. "Sometimes my brother's friends wanna chill, but they tell him not to bring me." When saying this we could hear the void and hurt in his voice. The biggest struggle he claims to have as a homeless adult is feeling sorry for himself. Even though his family may treat him wrong, Damien worries the most about his family. "I wanna make sure they alright."

Regardless of where he goes, Damien carries identification, social security card, his "right-hand man card" (work card), money, and his cell phone. A typical day for Damien is, as he says it, "normal." "I wake up, go to work, eat lunch, go to work, then go to sleep." Damien gets the majority of his sleep on weekends when he is not working. On his days off, Damien gets his lunch from the Liverpool on Central Avenue including "hamburgers, chicken, fries, and the usual stuff." Damien notices "In the morning, homeless people will wake up early to get food from the Liverpool."

Personally, we would not classify Damien as a "homeless" person because he has ambitions and a place to stay. Yet, after the interview, before seeing his face, we still saw the unkempt hair. As advice to people to keep them from becoming homeless, Damien says: "save money when living with your parents to have enough to get what you need…a house. Rules and discipline are good for you. Stay with your parents until you get your own place."

"Stay In School"
By Alicia Greene and Shaneetra Chappell

When my partner and I first entered the Coalition, we were struck with both feelings of excitement and anxiety as we searched for a person to interview. We eventually came across a man sitting on the curb preaching emphatically about politics and society. My partner and I looked at each other and exclaimed, "That's our man!" He was as tall and as skinny as a newly planted tree, standing at almost six feet tall. He had a dark brown complexion and short, black hair. He was clean-cut and he looked to be in his mid-thirties. We then approached him and persuaded him to participate in our interview.

After accepting our invitation he began to share his story; he was very hyper and fidgety. He was very well-spoken, speaking fast and clearly like a car salesman as he pieced together his life for us. He maintained eye contact and gave us the impression that this was going to be an honest interview. He gave us a kind of "Listen to me because I know what I'm doing" vibe. He seemed very experienced; this is a man who knew what life was about. He also didn't seem like he acknowledged the other people at the Coalition as much as he did politics and social theory; he seemed to be very educated. He smiled the whole time that we questioned him, appearing to be excited to tell his story. He spoke of having children; he seemed like the type of father that was a friend to his kids and let the mom do the disciplining.

He was definitely the type of person a kid would look up to, especially if it was a boy. He stressed staying in school and avoiding boys because they'd get you in trouble; he seemed like the big-brother kind of dad. As my partner and I continued our interview, we realized that everybody in the Coalition has a story to tell.

This is Tim Browns' story....

I was born in Orlando on March 2nd, 1962. I moved to Philadelphia when I was six and didn't return to Orlando until 2006. I had a pretty good upbringing; I had three brothers and one sister and both of my parents were around and together. My mother was a nurse and my father was a chef. I loved my mother very much, she was the one who kept me active in school. I was the "baby boy," so I got the majority of the things I wanted. Ever since I was a young kid my aspirations were to be a chef. It was not because of my father, but because of the looks and smells of cooking; it intrigued me. I wanted a skill. I went to Germantown High and was very active in school with the help of my mother, but around my junior year girls and drugs started getting in the way and eventually caused me to leave high school.

I drank occasionally and would do drugs, but I wasn't what you would call an "addict" until my mother passed away when I was thirty. After that, my father cut off all communication with me and I became addicted to alcohol. The jobs that I had throughout my life after high school were all related to cooking and culinary work. At first, I worked at Gino's, which was a northern version of KFC. Eventually I began working at a Philadelphia airport catering to the airplanes; I also worked at a prison in Pennsylvania as a cooking instructor to the inmates. Soon after, my mother passed away and I moved to Atlantic City.

Meeting my wife, Tanya, changed my world for the better. She made me a better man and taught me how to be more responsible, because nobody wants to be with a troubled man; I was a troubled man, indeed. I had been to prison, robbed banks, and burglarized homes. I came back to Orlando because I was tired of family headaches. Tanya and I had to get away from it all. I finally received my GED after trying so many times. I went to the Orlando Culinary Arts School to get my trade certificate.

My biggest regret in life is not being responsible. I never paid my bills on time and I never had my priorities straight. Also, I regret letting alcohol run my life; I lost many good jobs because of that.

I have two daughters, Autumn, who is two and a half, and Aliyha, who is one year old. I also have another girl due in February. I'm very worried about my children being raised in this environment because the world today is much scarier than before. Also, here at the Coalition the children pass around germs and colds. However, it's not as harmful for our family as it is to others because we have medical insurance.

Other people do not treat me much differently because they are not aware that I am homeless. I have never been treated without respect, but that is because I never disrespect anyone. The police don't bother me either because I no longer live a troubled life. I don't view any of the other homeless people differently because I don't feel that any person is beneath anybody else. I believe all men are equal, or at least should be.

My wife is my support system and I know she will always be with me. She inspires me. I hope I can get a home for my family soon; not an apartment, but a house, and I want to start my own business.

"Stay in school. Get [yourself] a career. Stay away from negativity. Stay responsible. Do what you need to do. So basically, stay motivated and keep going to school and don't be influenced by others doing wrong things. Keep doing what you're doing. Stay focused. Leave boys alone, and the most important thing for me to pass onto you is, stay in school."

"Unpredictable Saturday"

By Sympson Placide

On a sunny Saturday, November 4th, 2006, we visited a homeless shelter in downtown Orlando. My peers and I went to the Coalition excited and curious, thinking that we were going to meet a bunch of helpless individuals. However, after interviewing two of the homeless men, my perception changed.

When we arrived they were all sitting as a group talking with each other. I was really impressed to see how vivacious they all were. Gary was the first person that I met. He was sitting on the concrete and accepted my invitation for an interview with a smile. Gary was born in Philadelphia, Pennsylvania. One of his aspirations in life was to become a truck driver like his father, which he accomplished. For a period of time he was a local truck driver for eighteen-wheelers and his life was going quite smoothly.

He soon got married and eventually had a family of five kids. They all live separately; one lives in Florida, while the other four live in Mississippi. Gary explained that he will never forget the memories he has of his kids. He had high hopes for them, but he was sent to jail for stealing cars.

As a child, Gary described himself as a carefree person who was very dedicated to school; however, he was unable to overcome the peer pressure he encountered as a teenager. He grew up in Philadelphia around kids who had a negative influence on him. Gary explained that during this period he thought that everything was perfect; he was considered a rebel by society and wouldn't take advice from anybody. He trusted only in friends who shared the same destructive mentality as himself.

Gary's mother and father were doing their jobs as parents. They both took care of him and provided for him; however, they did not have the time to watch him or discipline him when he did wrong. He expressed gratitude towards his parents because they tried to take care of him the best they could.

Gary explained to me that he learned from his mistakes and wanted to help out by giving the advice he refused to accept when he was younger. Since he experienced everything himself, he knows how important it is to make the right decisions in life. He explained that in order to prevent a regretful life, one should avoid using drugs and choose their friends carefully; being homeless is very unlikely if you follow his advice, he said.

He never gave up on having goals either. His goal is to one day have a positive impact on society where he can have a good job and help his kids prepare for their future. He says that everybody needs a second chance.

I also had the opportunity to interview Floyd, the second individual who I had met. He was a very wise looking man, covered in gray hair. Floyd was born and raised in Louisiana with thirteen brothers and sisters. His parents were financially incapable of providing for the entire family. However, he told me that his family was always happy and supportive of each other. They all live in separate states, including Louisiana, Texas, California, and Washington. They all keep in touch.

Floyd still remembers a lot from his childhood. He said that he always had a lot of fun with his brothers and learned a lot from them. They lived exciting childhoods. One of his brothers, who he was the closest to, passed away at the age of twenty-two; he left behind a son in Texas.

Floyd dropped out of high school in tenth grade. He started doing drugs and explained to me that drugs were the one main influence that ruined his life and put him in his unfortunate situation. He had been put in jail for ten years because of drugs. He explained that he tried to quit, but he was never able to extinguish his habit. One of his short-term goals is defeating his addiction.

"Treat Others As You Would Like to Be Treated"
By Malaika Joseph and Natacha Pompilus

Natacha and I interviewed a man by the name of Guy S. Dume. He was born in Port-au-Prince, Haiti, and raised in Miami, Florida. He came to America as a boy with a family of seven children. He speaks English better than his native language, Creole.

As a young boy, Guy was very interested in school. After graduating from high school, he went to trade school. He hasn't finished college, but school has been great for him so far. Guy used to work at Universal Studios in

Orlando. He has a lot on his mind and a lot to say; he is very comfortable talking about his life and his past.

Guy does not do drugs or drink alcohol. He states that he was homeless because of a "political issue." He has been homeless for five months now and refused to talk about his family. Whenever we would inquire about his family, he would tell us that he didn't want to talk about it. He did say that his dream when he was younger was to get married and have kids, which he did. After being homeless, he started to lose contact with his wife and son. He said that his wife was very upset with him. He explained that the biggest challenge he has as an adult is being homeless and living at the shelter.

At the Coalition, Guy sleeps on average for about six hours on the floor. He explained that he doesn't care where he is, he just needs to keep an eye on the people around him. He said that he doesn't trust anybody at the shelter because they steal his money and take his clothes. He told us that he has to pay $1 to stay at the shelter every night; if he doesn't have the money he must stay outside.

He is a very confident, sociable, and happy man. He supports himself by working for a staffing company. His advice to others is to go on with life as you wish. Being homeless is not the end of the world. Guy said, "Everyone has the right to do things. Look at life as a back up. Go with what you have." His slogan was: *"Treat others as you want to be treated."*

```
**The Coalition clarified that they do not turn anyone away for not
having $1; they have plenty of chores around and offer
everyone the opportunity to do a chore in lieu
of the $1 fee.
```

"Can You Really Tell?"
By Kerline Delva

Small, large, short, tall, does the shape matter? Black, white, brown, tan, does the color matter? Can you really tell who the person is by the way they look? Can you tell by the way they talk, the way they walk? Is homeless a word that is known, or is it in a box that needs to be opened? How many people are living their lives not knowing what's going to happen the next day, hour, or even the next minute? Sitting down reflecting, how can this happen to me? What would I do if people looked down on me? That's how Shawn felt at the age of thirty-two.

Born in Orlando, Florida on May 24, 1974, with no father in sight, everything started out rough for Shawn. His mother's boyfriend was like the father that he never had. Shawn later found out that he should have thought twice. A man he doesn't know was beating on him and his mother. He wanted to do something but he was too weak and too young to defend himself and his mother. He couldn't do anything but cry and cry until his mother couldn't take it anymore. She gave him up for adoption at the age of four, something he thought would never happen. Without a mother, his life went down hill.

He traveled from foster home to foster home not knowing what was going to happen next. He saw horrible things. He felt lonely and needed a mother and father to love. How would you feel at the age of four not knowing where your mother or father is, asking yourself, "Why am I still living?" and "Does anybody love me?" He finally settled with a foster mother that took good care of him until the age of fourteen. Shawn did not have a father figure in his life, so he followed his older brother who was also living the street life. He began smoking marijuana at the age of fourteen, getting into trouble in school, and not attending class; that was what his older brother did. He knew it was wrong, but he wanted to fit in with the crowd, any crowd. He wanted to impress his friends and his brother so he could be important.

Going to school was quite difficult for him. As much as he wanted to overcome the addiction of smoking marijuana, his friends were always influencing him to do it more and more. Peer pressure and poor school attendance contributed to him being educated on the streets, and what an education that turned out to be. At the age of nineteen he was injured by a friend over a girl that meant nothing but trouble. He was convicted of four felonies, became a thief, drug abuser, and was incarcerated. He eventually ended up in another form of foster home, jail. After he was released, he ended up living with a friend and his friend's wife in an apartment. During this short period of time, his friend was going through a divorce with his wife and Shawn was forced to leave. Where could he go? He didn't know so he became homeless.

Today he is in a drug and alcohol free program that provides him with more advantages than other homeless addicts. He lives at the Coalition under the supervision of this program. Soon he will be able to help other people out while remaining drug and alcohol free. Shawn has been living in the Coalition for a month and a half trying to make something of his life by being clean and free in his mind, body, and soul. His dreams and aspirations are to receive his GED and to become a graphic designer so he can create his own artwork which would be given to charity instead of being sold. To him it's a way to give back to the community and knowing that he had a chance to make a difference. Hopefully this will not be a negative path, but finally a positive one for Shawn.

"God Has a Plan for All of Us"
By Bionca Bachelor

"Feed your faith and your fears will starve to death." This is the way Chesarae lives her life in a society that looks down on her. Through all of her trials and tribulations, and sometimes uncertainty, disbelief is never an option because she believes that "God has a plan for all of us". Chesarae, like most of us, lived a life where both parents were involved and love was always in arms reach. She had dreams that any normal person would have about things she wanted to do in life. Of all those dreams she never dreamed of being homeless.

As a child Chesarae was really energetic and craved attention. She enjoyed attending school even though she was constantly picked on by her peers because she didn't have all the fortunes they were blessed with. After she completed the eighth grade other things started to distract her, such as marijuana and friends. Afterwards, despair quickly entered Chesarae's world. Being arrested once and only wanting to hang with friends and indulge in marijuana, Chesarae quickly began to miss out on chances in life.

Fears are most people's downfall or biggest enemy because they don't know how to get rid of them, but Chesarae has a method that I think is awesome and the best way to live by; she has FAITH. Chesarae has fears of not being able to be a good mother for her children and she fears the world that is outside of the homeless life because she knows that one day her children will have to face it. But she doesn't let it get her down because she serves a God that is greater than any human or troubles she has come into contact with.

Chesarae's everyday life consists of breakfast at McDonalds, an appointment with her doctor to check on her upcoming baby, lunch at wherever she happens to be at the time, playtime with the daughter she so desperately wants to raise properly, and dinner at the shelter. Right now being homeless is not an obligation, it's a choice for Chesarae. This is a result of her being irresponsible and abusing drugs. She is taking life step by step with her family, saving money so that she and her husband can move on to something better.

She would say, "Being homeless is not the end of the world." Chesarae deals with illnesses such as asthma, colds, and the flu but has normal checkups. She has a family that consists of her husband, daughter, son, and the baby that she is expecting. Her son is in a foster home but they still keep in contact.

Chesarae is a stay-at-home mom who has been a cashier, bartender, and a worker in a warehouse. She takes pride in her children and her love for God which she feels is her savior. And even though Chesarae feels like she could have done a lot of things differently, like be more responsible with money, she has no regrets because she feels that "God has taken her through the storms for a purpose."

As of now, Chesarae's goals in life are being the best mom that she can be, staying involved in her children's life, and staying dedicated to God in order to go to heaven. I believe she will accomplish these goals because "having the ability to overcome trials and tribulations is the best victory of them all. God bless!"

"The Untouchable"
By Rayiaz Khan

In our society they are the homeless, impoverished and poor; Indians would call them the untouchables. They are the people we do not even glance at, and when we do, we scorn at the sight of them. Who are they, begging for money? They had all the chances. They could have had the same opportunities as we did, but they probably wasted those chances in order to get more booze and smokes. This is the stereotype that many people believe and, until recently, what I believed. That changed when I met Tera

Baker and her daughter Ashley, two kind and compassionate people who got the short end of the stick, so to say.

Tera Baker was born in Miami, Florida, but she did not remain there long. She moved to Gainesville, Florida, where she later had her daughter Ashley. She was married for five years to her ex-husband and within this time had five kids who still live with her. Tera believes that she was unable to reach all of her goals in life because she got married and had to raise a family early on. While she hasn't had any problems with alcohol or drugs, she has run into problems with the law. Once she received a check in the mail that was for the previous owner of the house and instead of sending it back, she cashed it and kept the money as hers. This resulted in her spending some time in jail.

She has many fond memories of her early life and of her parents. She was brought up by both of her parents, but preferred her mother over her father. She remembers her mom as a very happy person who loved to sing. Once, when they first moved into a new house, her mom was forced to use the fireplace as a stove; this was hilarious to her. She remembers her and her sister venturing off into the forest with the neighborhood kids, building a fort and pretending they drank coffee like Ms. Baker's dad. She also remembers going to Hardees and helping her dad clean up the place. In exchange for helping her dad, she would get unlimited drinks from the soda fountain for free. Ms. Baker can recall one memory she was especially fond of; whenever she was walking around the dirt road near her house, she would pretend she was driving on the road as a bus driver. This led to one of her many jobs.

In her life, Ms. Baker has worn the hats of many professions. She's been a waitress, bus driver, taxi driver, teaching assistant, substitute teacher, and newspaper carrier. From all of these jobs the one she's liked the most is her job as a teaching assistant. This is due to her love of learning and teaching others. She hopes to become a teacher and is trying to make this dream a reality by going to Valencia Community College so that she can get a college degree. In addition to majoring in Education, she wants to minor in Business. Therefore, she can have something to fall back on in case things don't pan out in education.

How did Ms. Baker become destitute? A combination of bills and the loss of one of her sources of income contributed to her becoming poverty stricken. With the separation of her husband, she was forced to support herself and her children. Paying the bills soon became a hard obstacle to overcome. To make matters worse, her son lost his SSI check which finally tipped the scales and forced Ms. Baker and her family to move into the coalition.

Since moving into the Coalition, things have been getting better for the Bakers. They have a place to live and are slowly rebuilding their lives. Ms. Baker is especially appreciative to the Coalition since they didn't split up her family; her son is over 18 so he should live separately from the rest of the family, but the Coalition allowed this to slide. Also, she's benefited from the many programs offered there and the tight knit support group at the Coalition. She feels at home there since everyone is in the same boat.

While this family has had misfortunes, this has not stopped them from being optimistic and constantly pushing themselves forward. As Ms. Baker said, "Work hard to depend on yourself."

"Mr. Bob"
By Ruth Cherubin and Frances Fignole

The life of Mr. Bob, or "Bob" as he prefers to be called, started like anyone else's life. He was an honor student and a high school graduate, and he attended sporting events like basketball and baseball. He was even enrolled in college for a year. Like most people, he gets teary-eyed; his first kiss was late at night under a mulberry bush. Unfortunately, due to bad influences and his lack of self control, his life took a turn for the worst when he became involved in drugs and alcohol; it was a memory which hasn't faded or been forgotten.

Born on the 7th of July, 1953 and raised by his mom and dad, Mr. Bob was a child who had a lot of expectations. He was a good child and was very shy, quiet, and intelligent. Mr. Bob had a good relationship with his mom since she was the one who understood him. He remembers his mom's efforts and struggles to prepare picnics and Christmas. As a teen, he wanted to become someone successful. He wanted to work in a car factory; if not he could be a printer. After completing his academic years in a vocational high school he wanted to attend a university. He took computer classes during the first year, then stopped going. However, he realized that such a decision hurt him since he achieved little after those days.

After his mother passed away, he decided to leave his hometown and move to Florida since he had a relative there and the temperature was moderate for him. While in Florida, he moved in with his aunt. He soon moved out because he didn't like living alone with her. Since he had no other family members, he was left on his own and had to face the real world with very little; it seemed like nothing. He could've moved to Boston with his sister but refused because it was too cold. He thought the weather would make him sick.

Mr. Bob is single; he has no children of his own and has not gotten involved in any relationships. He believes that his unspeakable way of life will never reach any woman's expectations. His addiction to alcohol caused him to have inconsistent jobs, making it difficult to make enough money to meet his needs. Therefore he had to live in a homeless shelter to help him with his troubles and endure discrimination for who he is. He believes he has no value in the eyes of many others: "As I recall, I was once attacked to my amazement. I pulled through and I'm still here". He added, "In the eyes of the police I am like a drug dealer, someone who doesn't belong."

Mr. Bob sleeps from 9:00 pm to 7:00 am in the morning; more often than not he sleeps on the floor. He tried to find a job and do some other things just to earn some money. Wherever he goes, he always carries his blanket and his clothes since it might get stolen. Mr. Bob believes that things are the way they are supposed to be, even though he has been living in the homeless shelter for only three months. He points out that they should be treated with better care and be respected like any other. He also notices that such an environment should not be for kids since it is not a good environment to raise a young one.

Mr. Bob receives medical care once a week and has his own psychiatrist to assist with his mental illnesses. What he wants is to be considered as an equal and treated with respect. He also wants to have a place to stay and a job. Eventually he wants to meet someone and make enough money to support himself. To achieve his goal, he believes that money and support from family will lead him there. He wants to have a dream house located near the beach and a '65 Ford Mustang.

Mr. Bob has regretted a lot about his past life. He mentioned, "I have a lot of regrets, especially for drinking and smoking. I should've taken my job more seriously and finished my computer class course." His advice for others is to get a good job, don't do drugs, and stay close to our family members. "Life offers a lot. It's your job to benefit from it and take every opportunity that passes by."

"It's Easy to Do Wrong"
By Fabienne Elie

Jovial, warm, and funny are the words I would use to describe John Hawk. He reminded me of one of those bodyguards we usually see on TV. He's taller than the average person and he's black. He even had the round belly, but unlike the bodyguards, he wasn't wearing a suit. He was wearing a plain white shirt, a pair of blue jeans, and black shoes. He didn't have a beard but he looked like he hadn't shaved in a while. When he walked up to us, it felt like the whole room had brightened somehow. With him he brought a vibrant presence, a fun-loving character, and his memories. As we talked, I kept feeling like he was trying to hide things from me. He seemed to conceal his deepest feelings behind his smiles and his laughs.

Born in New York, John lived with his parents until he was fifteen. He grew up in a good familial environment where he felt loved. He and his parents had good communication and they were always there for him. They encouraged him to stay in school but he didn't; he dropped out of school when he was in tenth grade and started hustling and selling drugs. He became rebellious and left his parents' house. He went to live with other family members in North Carolina but, after a while, they kicked him out. After, he went back to his parents' house. Aside form New York and North Carolina, John also lived in Ohio, Pennsylvania, and Washington.

John's decision to drop out of high school cost him more than he had expected. He left because things started going badly for him as he started high school: peer pressure, more work, more stress... I guess he thought he couldn't handle it. Unfortunately things became worse after he began to spend more time in the streets; he was sent to prison three times. He spent five years in prison the first time and one year the second. The third time he was arrested for selling drugs and stayed in prison for ninety days. For someone who has gotten into so much trouble, the fact that he now worries about always doing the right thing is incredible. When I asked him why he replied, "it's easy to do wrong."

When he was a child, he had wanted to become a cop because they had guns. Now, he hates people with authority. He's not married and he doesn't have any children. So his happiest moments in life do not include the birth of his child or his marriage. Instead, the most ecstatic moment of his life is the time when he got out of prison. He's grateful to be alive and he feels happy every time he realizes he's still breathing and that he has been granted another day.

John is not the kind of person who cares too much about what people think. In fact, he doesn't care at all! However, he knows that people try to judge him when they see him, even though most of these people do not even know him. Although he dropped out of school when he was a teenager, he's making better decisions concerning his education. For instance, he has gone back to school and is now trying to obtain his GED and become a heavy equipment operator. What kind of help does he need from us to help him accomplish his goals? None, except our moral support. I would have expected him to be more bitter or rude because he was in a bad situation and here I was asking him to talk to me about his ordeal and to share with me why or how he became homeless. Instead, he struck me as a friendly person. His advice to the youth of America is to listen to their loved ones because, more often than not, they're usually right. Yet one thing that will predominantly come to my mind whenever I think of him is not his smile, but what he kept saying throughout the whole interview: "I chose to be homeless."

Why would he *choose* to be homeless in the first place? His comment made me think that he was lying and that there are some choices he made that led to his homelessness but he preferred to think he didn't regret them. Or maybe he thought we would feel sorry for him if he told us the truth. I don't think he really likes having nowhere to go and always having to worry about what he will do tomorrow. I do not believe anybody chooses to be homeless. Something always happens that causes situations to go from bad to worse. A person usually does not become homeless just because he wants to. Even if he did, something must have happened that caused him to make such a choice.

Yet, John does not spend every moment of his life thinking, "maybe if I hadn't done this or that, or maybe if this had not happened I wouldn't be here right now." If he did, he would not smile as often as he did. In fact, he was laughing during our whole conversation and the fact that he was even able to laugh when he didn't know where his next meal would come from or what tomorrow would entail really surprised me.

"Linnie Johnson"

By: Tiffany Walker and Eveline Joachim

"Father always told me to be a lady," said Linnie Johnson. Never in a million years would you think that being a lady would result in prostitution, but to Linnie Johnson it did. Linnie Johnson was born in Augusta, Georgia, August 5, 1939. Born to Johnny and Emma Carry Lou Johnson, Linnie grew up in the segregated south. She loved school, waking up every morning at 3:00 am by a rooster. She would begin her day eating breakfast and heading out to her school bus by 6:00 am. Linnie explained that school wasn't too hard because her mother had taught her a lot before she started school; however, that experience didn't serve her well because she later dropped out of school after the eleventh grade.

At the age of twelve Linnie started drinking; it was the same year her father died of a stroke. Later on, after Linnie turned 19, her mother died of heart trouble. From this point Linnie was on her own. She began by getting a job at Krispy Kreme Donuts. After that she got a job in house cleaning. Not long after Linnie married a man named Ross Earl Randolph who she thought was "the right one." During this marriage she had three children, two girls and one boy. To Linnie Johnson this marriage was the beginning of her downfall; during this eleven year marriage her husband became very abusive and they got into many altercations. During this abusive relationship Ross hit Linnie so hard that her teeth fell out.

After Linnie had enough she left her husband. She then began to sell her body by becoming a prostitute to support her children. After the first three months of prostitution, Linnie was caught and put into jail, but this didn't stop her. This went on for as long as it could. By age 36 Linnie had given up her children to her older sister. This is the point where it all started, the state of being homeless.

Linnie has been homeless for 30 years now. At age 60 Linnie moved to Orlando, Florida and has been staying in a homeless shelter for six years. Linnie is still involved in prostitution. In fact, over the past 30 years Linnie has slept with over 900 men. She hardly ever gets any sleep. There have been times where she has not slept in a whole week. When she sleeps, she sleeps in a Laundromat. She eats food at the homeless shelter and eats breakfast every Wednesday at New Destiny Church. She showers at people's houses and keeps her belongings at her friend's house. Linnie only gets her medical care when she goes to jail. She has multiple illnesses that she inherited from her parents; seizures, strokes, heart trouble, and diabetes. At age 66 Linnie Johnson's Goal is to get off of the streets. She has no regrets in life and no fears in life because she is "trusting in the Lord". Linnie's advice to younger girls is to stay independent and work.

"Kelvina"

By Tiffany Walker and Eveline Joachim

Most people become homeless because of the law, drugs, or alcohol, but in Kelvina Coleman's case that is not so. Sometimes financial hardships just can't be overcome, as Kelvina and her children discovered.

Kelvina Coleman was born in Clearwater, Florida February 17, 1968. Growing up as a child, Kelvina described herself as a loner craving for attention. She was involved in different clubs, but one that stood out the most to Kelvina was chorus. Her childhood dream was to be a singer, but unfortunately she didn't achieve this goal. She didn't have the support that she needed and longed for. Kelvina went on with school, but only completed the eleventh grade. After, she quit school and moved to Fort Myers where she began a new life.

At the age of 18, Kelvina got married. She also found a job working with handicap children. Everything was going well until one day Kelvina found out that the man she married was gay and was cheating with her male best friend. Eleven years of marriage down the drain. Several years after her divorce, at the age of 32, Kelvina had her first child. Now at the age of 38 she has four children ages 7, 5, and 2-year old twins. Kelvina has no relationship with her family; all she has is her children. She has a love that flows deep for her children. She's just happy to wake up with them everyday.

Kelvina is now living in a shelter where she and her children have lived for a month now. They were forced into the shelter because the place where they were living was remodeled and the rent went up. Kelvina simply didn't have enough time to find another place to stay so she moved to a shelter. As Kelvina points out, it is very stressful to try to raise kids and live without a home. Kelvina has no struggles with drugs or alcohol. In fact, she has never been in trouble with the law. According to her, "anybody could become homeless." Living in a homeless shelter, Kelvina has to put her family belongings in lockers. They only get about five or six hours of sleep and they sleep in dorms. The shelter provides breakfast, lunch, and dinner. Kelvina gets medical care every six months at Orange Blossom Clinic.

"There are no dangers of being homeless," said Kelvina. Actually, homeless people are just like regular people. Kelvina's current goals are to get out of the shelter, return to church, and start singing again. She will do this with God's support. The advice to young teenagers is to stay strong, keep your head up, proceed with your dreams, and don't let anyone get in your way.

"The Dream Of A Woman Filled With Hope"
By Moise Civil and Gemima Louis

The following tells the story of a woman whose life has not been a great success. Even though she has found herself living in a world where hope is thought to have vanished, she builds a dream with a heart full of hope.

With little memory of her native state New York, she remembers traveling back and forth from New York, South Carolina, and Florida during her childhood. Raised by a single mother who did her best to provide for her, she left school and entered the workforce. Early in life she became a mother and now has five children and a husband of five years. She also remains in contact with her mother. "I contact her once a week," she says.

As a child she wanted to become a singer, but like many of us her childhood dream did not turn into a reality. From childhood to adulthood, one of her greatest jubilations was giving birth. However, her greatest challenge has been raising her children. From her experiences comes a message she wants to share with the rest of the world. She feels that everyone needs to go to school; not finishing school, especially college, is one mistake that she deeply regrets in her life.

When it comes to her children, spending is her middle name. When one of them desires something, she provides it for them without consideration of her budget or her bills (mortgage, phone, electricity and water.) As a result, she has found herself at the homeless shelter. It has been three weeks since she became homeless.

She wakes up in the morning, helps the kids get ready for school, does her chores in her surroundings, takes her younger kids to the park, and at the end of the day, reads a book before going to bed for six hours of sleep. As for her daily diet, she eats many different kinds of food.

During her three weeks staying at the homeless shelter, she has made some observations about the people around her and the surrounding environment. She believes that they are still ignorant of the lessons that life is trying to teach them; they still mismanage their budget, steal, and gossip. However, those are not the things she worries about. She worries mostly about the future of her children. She wants all the people who think of the homeless as disgraceful to know that homelessness could happen to anyone. They are not the worst individuals that exist. "We still hold on to our dreams," she says. Despite all of her hardships, she feels grateful for the medical care that she is able to obtain whenever she has the need for medical assistance.

Part of her vivacious dream is to one day own a restaurant; she is a great chef. She also hopes to start a clothing line and be a reality talk show agent. Her hopes along with her skills have helped turn her dream into a goal, which she is now working toward with all her strength. At this moment, she has someone doing her business proposal for her and is saving her salary; she plans on getting a loan so she can reach her goals. She wishes to show the world all the struggles she has overcome in a reality show. To begin her project, she expects the support of only two people: God and her husband. Overall, she has a nonchalant attitude; at the same time she is also very outspoken and straightforward. For her final words she tells us, "Never give up on your dreams and put your pride aside."

"Frank D. Crosby"
By Tiffany Longjohn and Serenitye Massey

As we walked to the picnic table in the courtyard, a man greeted us with a bright smile and grayish-blue eyes. He was a mature man with dirty-blonde hair. The feelings my partner and I had were overwhelming, but fear quickly left us as his calm face met ours. My partner and I opened our ears and eyes to a story unlike one we had ever heard before. It was Frank's story.

Q: What can you tell us about where you were born?
A: I was born in New Smyrna Beach, Florida in the cold fall. I am the only child in my family.

Q: Where else have you lived during your lifetime?
A: I have lived in Orlando for 10 years. I was also in the NAVY so I traveled other places as well.

Q: Who raised you? What do you remember most about them?

A: I was raised by my father. I remember him being a heavy smoker and an alcoholic.

Q: What were you aspirations/dreams as a child?

A: I wanted to go into the military, the Navy to be more specific. It was sort of a family tradition.

Q: What do you remember about your childhood?

A: When I was a child I was in slow education. I remember I started kindergarten in 1977 at the age of six. I went to Grand Elementary in New Smyrna Beach.

Q: How would you describe yourself as a child?

A: I was an upset child. I almost died at the age of six. I overdosed on some drugs and almost lost my life. (**Sadly looks down**)

Q: What is the highest level of school you have attained?

A: Well I attended high school and college. I graduated in 1991. After that I worked two jobs from 1993-1995. I was a service agent. Then I moved and enlisted in the NAVY in 1998.

Q: What were some jobs that you had?

A: Well you know I was a service agent. I also was a data entry specialist. Umm... Let's see, a dishwasher for a restaurant, a construction worker, a digger, and a traffic director.

Q: Have you ever been married?

A: No, I have never been married. I wanted to get married before I turned 40, but that does not seem like it's going to happen **(laughs).**

Q: Do you have any children?
A: No. I don't have children...yet **(smile)**.

Q: Do you still maintain a relationship with your family? By what means and how often?
A: No... I don't talk to them very often **(frown)**. However when I do talk to them it is by telephone.

Q: What have been two of your happiest moments as an adult?
A: I would have to say visiting California and going to the Navy for four years. California was beautiful, probably one of my favorite places.

Q: What have been two of your biggest challenges as an adult?
A: One of my struggles would have to be trying to get married before forty and the other would be trying to create a better lifestyle for myself.

Q: Have you ever struggled with drugs or alcohol?

A: No. I have not done any drugs unless it was a prescription from a doctor and well…drinking… a little here and there but it has never been a problem.

Q: Have you ever been in trouble with the law? How has this impacted your life?

A: Yes. I was sleeping somewhere that I shouldn't have been but it was cold that night. They came and took me to 33rd street. I was in jail for 62 hours. I thought different of the police after that.

Q: Do you have any regrets?

A: Yes. Not having kids and not having a better life**.**

Q: What do you worry most about?

A: I worry about death the most. I feel at this point in my life that I am going to die alone. That scares me.

Q: How long have you been homeless?

A: I would have to say about eight years now.

Q: What is a typical day for you like how many hours do you get of sleep?

A: Well I get about eight hours of sleep and of course I sleep at the coalition shelter. I have about two or three friends I talk to during the day. For lunch and stuff I usually eat sandwiches which are ok.

Q: Speaking of friends, how do you feel they treat you here? Do you have a lot of friends?

A: Most are lazy bums. They don't want to work and they are not trying to find a job. My life has been threatened here twice and someone stole my mat one time. My friends are cool but I can't say I relate to these people, no.

Q: What are your current goals in life?

A: My current goals right now are to get married, start a better life, and get out of this place. I mean get out of being homeless.

Q: Ok. So if you were living out your dream today what would it be?

A: I would get out of Florida and move to the dessert regions. I would hook up to the Internet and just chill... you know a little R and R, rest and relaxation.

Q: Do you have any advice for us?

A: Just stay in school and get a successful job. Maintain communication with your loved ones and remain in good health.

We go on to speak about war and the education system. He was very down to earth and just seemed to have peace within him even though he knew he was in a stiff situation. The experience for my partner and I was satisfying and made us really appreciate where we were in life. We will never forget the day Frank Crosby told us his story.

"Momma's Always There"

By Fanancy Doralus and Natasha Daverman

It was a windy and early Saturday afternoon. There were concrete floors and a smelly urine musk that hung in the air as we walked through the unclean entrance. Many people were staring as we passed by, others were walking around aimlessly. Children were playing around. When we walked through, we did not know how people would react to us. Some were friendly and smiling, while others were confused.

We walked around trying to find a person to interview. Some didn't want to, some had already been interviewed, and a few did not even speak English. Ileana Cruz stood out in a crowd because she looked determined, as if she did not belong there. Her dark curly hair and angelic smile caught our eyes instantly. "I haven't been interviewed yet," she said as she grabbed her children and her husband and joined us at the picnic table. She was more than open and anxious to share her story with us.

Ileana was born on May 16, 1983 in Hartford, Connecticut. She grew up in a predominately Hispanic community surrounded by violence, gang-bangers, robberies, shoot-outs, killings, etc. "Living next to gang-bangers wasn't the best place to live." At the age of seven, Ileana's parents divorced. Her mother gained custody of Ileana and her two siblings. Ileana described her mother as a strict, traditional Puerto Rican school teacher. Born in Puerto Rico, Ileana's mother held on to the traditional customs of her culture. Her parents believed in physical abuse as a way of discipline for their children; it was meant to encourage them to do their best.

Although Ileana lived with her mother, she felt as if she was raising herself. She described her relationship with her mother as "not good". "Our relationship is rocky. It's good and bad. We have communication issues. Even now, as an adult, she still feels the need to control my life." When asked about her father, Ileana described her father as "a sick man." Ileana's father was not around much as she grew up. The few times that he was there he brought torment for her and her siblings. He would abuse them verbally and physically, beating them with anything he could get his hands on. Ileana recalled being bruised by phone cords, branches, shoes, and leather belts. "He was a social worker. Not a great father figure; he wasn't there for my siblings and I while we were growing up." She also included that he did not provide them with child support. "Nothing."

Being the youngest of three children, Ileana had few playmates. She was a timid child who kept to herself, with big plans. At home she established the role of "permanent babysitter" for her older sister who by the age of 19 already had her second child. With a house filled with people, Ileana felt all alone. Her refuge from home was school, the only place where she did not have to endure the hardship that occurred at home. Now, at the age of 23, Ileana still does not have a great relationship with her family. She says that she barely keeps in touch with her father and her siblings. "Me and my brother grew apart and my sister has a family of her own." Though they had their differences, Ileana mainly talks with her mother, "She's always there." The mother and daughter communicate through phone calls.

As a child, Ileana's passion was music. She dreamed of becoming a singer. During her spare time she took various singing classes, wrote lyrics and sang in her local church. Music is still her passion, the only thing that allows her to be creative.

Ileana's love for school was not great enough to keep her in. At the age of 17, before the beginning of her senior year in high school, Ileana dropped out, left home and went to live with her first boyfriend in Massachusetts. A year later, Ileana gave birth to her first child at the age of 18. After the birth of her son, Ileana's utopian relationship slowly started to fall apart. She was abused and beaten by her boyfriend, which eventually caused her to leave him. Ileana tried to get her life back on track. She went back to school and received her GED.

Throughout her life time, Ileana had obtained various jobs. She began as a tutor at the school where her mother was teaching. She went on to work at a circus; watching children play around in a play pen. She handed out gift bags, worked at J-Mart, sold Avon products and worked at hotels as a house keeper and lobby attendant.

Ileana had to overcome many obstacles in her life; including getting over a bad relationship, a bad drug habit, and drinking problem. She admitted to using drugs, "coke and weed" and to drinking hard liquor. "This was a struggle" she said, "It was not a good decision; a waste of my time and I could have used the money and saved up. I regret it...My biggest challenges in life has been raising my kids and to better myself. I don't regret my kids; I just regret the age that I had them…I wasn't prepared. I regret not finishing school." Though she had all of these problems, Ileana never had any contact with the law.

Ileana soon moved to Tampa, Florida and then to Orlando, Florida where she found her husband. When the subject of her husband and family came up, Ileana's face brightened. Ileana proclaimed that "the greatest moment of my life was when I got married and when I had my kids." Ileana met her husband, Victor Cruz, three years ago at the age of 19. Victor accepted Ileana and her son and eventually the couple had a son of their own. Victor had two daughters, ages 10 and 7, from a previous marriage whom he had not seen for over a month. It was obvious that Ileana and Victor were happy. Ileana described her life with her new husband as "Happy...He makes me feel comfortable, he is trustworthy. He's my best friend..."

Ileana and Victor were living a good life, they were living with friends and had food and shelter. After a while, their friend decided to sell the house without their consent. The friend did not bother to tell the couple until it was too late. Stranded, without any money, food, shelter, the family was forced to find means to get help. Ileana moved into the

Coalition with her children; a room with eighteen beds and filled with different types of people, while her husband, too proud to accept public assistance, tried to find a place to sleep. Eventually Victor moved into the Coalition with his wife and children where they have been living for the past month.

The family now lives in a "Family Room"; a room with four beds, tiny shelves, filled with all of their lively possessions: their clothes, legal papers, toys, shoes, and "whatever's donated", much more than they could carry if they had to pick up and leave.

Ileana shared with us her daily ritual. "I wake up at 5 am, that's if I want to be able to eat breakfast, get the kids ready and hurry to get some food. We feed the kids which takes some time, get back to the room and wait for our case manager to come by. Our case manager helps us to find out if we can get welfare, if there are any job possibilities, and help us find anything that can help us. I don't get a chance to actually sleep. I take naps, two or three hours per day; I get five hours at the most. We have to get lunch somewhere else because the shelter doesn't offer it here, usually at the "Daily Bread". When we come back we try to relax, one of us would stay with the kids while the other go look for any possible jobs. We sleep in one room and share everything with each other."

Throughout her day, Ileana never leaves her children. She explains that there are a lot of dangers at the Coalition. "People here may have diseases, infections. I'm scared that my kids can get sick. The screening process here isn't good. The toilets and showers aren't clean…We have no Medicare; we have to go to the free homeless clinic if we get sick…thank God we haven't had to go there once. " It was obvious that Ileana was stressed out. "There are good and bad people here. I keep to myself. There are some that I can relate to, others I can't. It depends on the person's personality and how they are. People misjudge you; they can be very gossipy or very nice.

The family's only source of income is from a few odd jobs that Victor manages to get. Ileana still receives child support from her first boyfriend but it's barely enough. "My family is my life. Everything I do is for them. My ambition keeps me going."

Ileana fears that one day she and her family will get out of this situation and eventually end back there. She dreams of going to college, becoming a masseuse, a hair stylist, and going to tech school the possibilities are endless. She is now going to night classes (refresher classes) that the Coalition offers. When asked, Ileana told us that her dream life is to have a beautiful house, with a swimming pool, two cars, nicer furniture, better clothes, and huge rooms for her children.

Ileana's last words for us were: "Being homeless is something that…something that happens that makes you homeless, there's always a reason and you shouldn't be treated differently because of it. If you have ambition, a goal, a dream, do it, don't think twice, do it! Stay in school, stay off of drugs, stay positive and do what you want to do no matter what."

"Daughter Of The Homeless"
By Vince Pham

Young, lively, outgoing, charismatic; these are just some of the words you could use to describe Ashley. She is the daughter of a kind and warm woman who hasn't been blessed with the best luck in the world. She's been forced to move into the Coalition for The Homeless. One would think that this girl would be depressed or unhappy. After all, she is homeless. But then you'd be wrong. She thrives on learning, constantly reading and writing, and most importantly dreaming.

Ashley loves to read, read, and read. She uses books not only to entertain herself, but also as vehicles to learn more about the world. She also said that books provide her with an escape away from the world. Her favorite genres include mystery, fiction, and non-fiction. This passion of reading has also inspired her to dream about beginning her own book publishing company when she becomes older.

School, like reading, is another passion for her. She loves to learn new things and have new experiences in life. She's been honored at her school for being one of the top three highest scorers on the FCAT standardized test. This is an honor that she is extremely proud of and still cherishes.

Ashley may be living in the homeless shelter, but she is making the most of her life. She is young and full of life with a passion for academics and reading. She is also a poet at heart and shared the following with me:

Lasted
By Ashley Baker

Joyfully screaming smiles are
Beaming from here to there
All everywhere I feel the breeze
I see the trees as they sway
From side to side I like ridding
The ridesl... I'm havin' a good
Time. But soon enough everyone's
Hiding and soon enough I am
Crying for I Am bored and
Then everyone's gone they are
Gone so long... so long and it
was fun while it lasted.

"A Regular Life"

By Calvin Hitnarain

What would you say about a person who had a regular life when they were young. Most people might say that person might be doing good for himself. Well, that's not the case for Otis. Otis was born in South Carolina. He was raised by his mother and grandmother. As he grew up, he lived in Nashville, Seattle, and now currently in Orlando. His mother and grandmother were the most regular people that he had known. They were like every other parent or guardian that took care of their kids and grandkids. They were very helpful especially when problems arose.

As a young boy growing up, his dream in life was to be rich, happy and to be the world's greatest harmonic player. Being the world's greatest harmonic player would bring "fame and fortune," and this he worried about because, he said, "too many people would come for him to get some money."

He went to school and completed his work like every other child. To Otis, school was the most important thing because without it there is no life. "Without an education you will not be able to become successful and be able to get what you want out of life."

In his life, Otis had many jobs but was never really able to keep them. He had jobs in supermarkets and small stores like most young people. Currently he does not have a job, but is looking for one so he could get back on his feet. The thing he needs and wants right now is "money in my pocket and a girl around my arm." He also wants to continue his dream to be the greatest harmonic player in the world. When we asked him if he could play us a tune, he said, "I can't I sold my harmonica." He sold his prize possession for money so that he could live another day. His advice to the young is not to do drugs and to stay in school. He states, "without drugs you can be focused on your academics and not what the world wants you to think about."

The next time you see a man on the side of the street who asks you for some money don't just walk away, maybe he is hitting a low point in his life. Don't think that the person only wants money to buy drugs. Really look at that person and think, "what if this was me?" Wouldn't you want someone to give you some money? Give a helping hand and you will get your reward even if it takes a while. Always remember that what happens to one person can also happen to you.

"Miguel"
By Thien Pham and Peterson Joseph

As Peterson and I walked along the path of the shelter, we saw people doing different kinds of things. There were people socializing, watching television, sleeping, reading books, listening to music, and relaxing. We were excited, but at the same time worried, about how to interview these people. Fortunately, we came upon a curious and willing man. He looked both anxious and friendly. As we greeted him, we knew that this was the person we wanted to interview. We sat down on the concrete path and began our interview. His name was Miguel Garcia and he was born in Mexico on April 13, 1960. Throughout his life, he traveled to many places such as New Jersey, New York, Pennsylvania, Indiana, Illinois, Alabama, Texas, Connecticut, and Florida. When he was in these places, he worked on construction, landscaping, and picking up oranges.

Miguel told us that his grandfather was a farmer, which explains why he had a little experience farming while he was a kid. Miguel's major dreams include attending school, playing basketball, and making the world a better place for hungry kids. Miguel wanted to attend school but his father thought it was a waste of time and wanted him to work. As a youngster, Miguel described himself as a hardworking, muscular, and adventurous person. Miguel told us that he once joined the army for three years in Panama and El Salvador. He got married at the age of twenty-two, remarried for five years, and divorced two years after. He has been raising his kids alone ever since. Even though Miguel did not have the chance to attend school, he thrived for success and would not forfeit. He knew that he had to work for himself and for the sake of his children in Mexico.

Miguel always wishes for his children to have an excellent education and an opportunity to do what they desire. Therefore, he would not quit; instead he would work constantly to provide money for his children. Miguel said he does not want his children to end up like him, waiting and working, but instead to create a brighter future of their own. Miguel said "Praise the Lord" for he still has contact and a good relationship with his son and daughter. His daughter is currently twenty-two years old and his son is twenty years old. As an adult, Miguel's happiest moments would be the time he spends with his friends drinking beer and socializing. He also smokes with his friends every once in a while. Even though Miguel smokes and drinks, he does not feel these things affect his life.

Miguel has not been in trouble with the law. Miguel usually sleeps from four to five hours a day and works early in the morning until night. When he arrived at the shelter in Orlando, he said, "This place is not really bad." Finally, Miguel got an opportunity to have more hours of sleep and less hours of work because he has not found a job yet. Miguel survived on bread, bacon, beans, and rice while he was at the shelter. Sometimes he drinks coffee and most of the time he carries a bottle of water along his journey. So far, he has not encountered any dangers while residing at the shelter. Miguel also has no problem with the people at the shelter, but sometimes he worries about meeting people in public. Since Miguel only arrived at the shelter one week ago, he has not sought out any medical care. Waiting for an appointment and acquiring a job would be Miguel's plans for the moment. The advice Miguel would want to offer to our youth group would be taking advantage of education because it will lead to a successful life.

The Life of a Homeless Man
By: Lencia Marc

To most people, the word "homeless" means people who are dirty, uneducated, stupid, drug addicts, and in trouble with the law. But those words do not describe every homeless person. Most of them are homeless because of a mistake they made or a bad choice that they made and they end up being homeless. Some of them have their high school diplomas and some even have college degrees. Some were successful, but they hung out with the wrong crowd. Some were born and raised poor. Like every normal person, they have goals and dreams to accomplish before they die.

The gentleman that I interviewed was born at the University Hospital in Birmingham, Alabama on December 18th 1940. His name is Raymond. He did not live in Birmingham for a long time. He moved to Chicago at a very young age. His aunt raised him in Chicago. He said his aunt raised him "with goat milk". When I ask him what he remembered about his mother and father, he did not say much, but he did say that she was "nice" and he was "alright." When he was saying these two words I could see that he was sad.

Mr. Raymond said what he remembers about his childhood was "working all the time". While he was young, he worked at a pawnshop, he was a butter man and he was head dishwasher at a hotel. He said he was an excellent child. He said he felt good about school and when he was in school he ran track and played football. His favorite subject in school was science. He obtained a high school diploma and that is the highest level of education he has attained. While he was talking about the different jobs that he had as a young man, he was sad. But when he was talking about school and the sports that he played, he seemed content.

After he graduated high school, he got a job as a construction worker. He has had many jobs and he shared some of them with me. Some of the fields that he has worked on are as followed: construction, steel corporation, roof company, restaurant and gas pump attendant. The only things they have in common are that they are all in Chicago.

Mr. Raymond had been married once for a year. According to him, the marriage ended because it did not come out good. He has a child, a son, to be more specific, with his ex-wife. He still maintains a relationship with his family, but he did not tell me how he did that. When I asked him what has been one of his happiest moments as an adult, he said, working and solving the problems. The biggest challenge as an adult for him is the things that he had to struggle with. He has never struggle with drugs, never been in trouble with the law, and have no regrets.

The thing that Mr. Raymond worries most about is not having a job. He has been homeless for one year and 6 months. He thinks that the thing that caused him to become homeless is being unemployed.

Here is how a typical day goes for Mr. Raymond. He usually sleeps for 8 hours at the shelter. During the day, he sometimes eats sandwiches, chicken, or anything else that they serve at the shelter. His belongings consist of clothes, and he is able to carry them all with him. He said he has never encountered any danger while being homeless. He told me that he can't relate to the other homeless people that are living in the shelter. Because they are not the same kind of people. He said he is not able to seek medical care. He told me he doesn't have to deal with illnesses because he doesn't get sick often. The money that he has right now, he gets them from working.

He said he feels like the police and other people treat him alright. His current goal in life is to buy a house. One thing that he's working on now to make this goal work is filling out job applications. He thinks that a loan would help him buy the house.

According to Mr. Raymond, if he was living the life of his dreams today it would be a good life. The advice that he would like to give to people, especially the youth, that might help keep them out of homelessness is don't waste your money.

After I left the shelter, I look at homeless people that I see on the streets very differently than before. Now, I don't look at them as a person that's a drug addict, stupid, uneducated, and who doesn't know how to clean themselves. I look at them as someone that made a few of bad mistakes that landed them on the streets.

"A Better Path"

By: Tuyen Pham and Vina Nguyen

How many people get a second chance? These days, once a person commits a crime they become outcasts. Jobs, places to live, family, and friends all become more difficult to acquire and keep when you become a criminal. Victor Cruz has had a life full of difficult choices. Victor is a very friendly, warm individual and speaks freely about his life. Many of us take our childhood for granted. Victor is someone that had to struggle and fight for everything he had. Born in New Jersey, Victor was always in trouble at school and at home. After getting into some trouble, Victor also joined a gang. At the age of 15, Victor was thrown in jail for the first time. This led to a path of hardship, uncertainty, and destruction.

After prison, Victor's mom decided to move to Florida hoping to it would get Victor out of trouble. They lived in Orlando for a short period of time. Victor hated being confined and wanted to travel. So, Victor traveled to many places including New York, Rhode Island, California, and Massachusetts. While in Massachusetts, Victor met his wife, Lleana. Lleana was born in Hartford Connecticut. A few years later their first child David Cruz was born. Two years after that, Victor and Lleana gave birth to a second child Victor Cruz Jr. Life was good for Victor and his family. Unfortunately, some events caused Victor to loose everything he had. He tries very hard to recreate life as he once knew it, but being homeless is complicated for Victor and his family. However, they still manage to struggle through their second chance in life. Victor doesn't get that much sleep, normally two hours a day. He is trying to make a way for his family. Victor considers being homeless the most disgraceful thing that could happen to a person. People treat him and his family badly. But no matter what, he still doesn't give up. He believes one day he will find a path to a better life for him and his family, even though he still struggles to find a job.

Victor has many regrets in life except for his family, which is the only thing that convinces him to try harder in life and to live one day at a time. He has a couple words of advice for the youth of today: "Take opportunities to be surrounded by your family and stay in school. Cherish it and don't give up."

"Females Are Better"
By: Duan Zirkle

As a young girl, everything seemed so innocent to Sara. Her father brought a new woman home every other month it seemed, but Sara didn't like any of them. Sara grew up not knowing her mother and was told by her father's parents that her mother had died. However, when Sara was four she learned that this was a lie. One day a woman came to her and told Sara that she was her mother. Sara believed her grandparents and told the woman that her mother was dead. She did not trust the woman, but the woman came back to visit her from time to time. Slowly the truth began to surface and the realization of the truth shattered the world Sara used to know.

Sara's mother was remarried to an American and was going through a court process to have Sara come to America with her. Because of her mother's new living conditions, the court entrusted Sara to her mother and they moved to America. In the beginning, life in America was miserable for Sara. She didn't have any friends and her classmates picked on her because of her race. She was always quiet because of her inability to speak English fluently. As time passed Sara learned to speak and understand English, but it wasn't for a long time that she understood why everything happened the way it did.

She eventually understood that because she was born a girl her grandparents made her father divorce her mother. Her father was the only son of the family so they wanted a grandson to pass on the family name. They also have the mindset that males are better than females. Upon realizing this, Sara worked hard in school because she wanted to prove to her grandparents that females can be better than males. Sara did not want to shame her mother either because her mother had supported her in so many ways. Sara's grades have been acknowledged by her school and her family, and every summer when she goes back to visit China her father would come and see her. Yet she feels a distance between them because she dislikes his weakness, uncertainty, and the lack of determination a man should possess.

Presently, Sara is one of the top four junior students at her school. She also has many other accomplishments, such as being in the National Honor Society and on the National Honor Roll. Not only does she participate in academic clubs, but she also plays on the school tennis team even though it's not that well-known of a team. Sara is also enrolled in all honors and AP classes. She also has a little side job; every summer when she goes to China for vacation she tutors her cousins or family friend's child in English. Sara dreams of becoming a doctor not only because it is a respectful occupation where she gets to save lives, but also because it would show her father and grandparents that she, even as a young woman, could do anything she puts her mind to.

"Control Your Destiny"

By Wisnerson Benoit and Laurel Liburd

So you take your first breath and then what? All we can do is take what is handed to us and try to make something out of it. That's exactly what Tim did. "I was eight when I realized what life was really about," Tim said to me as we began an interview that would change the way we would view life forever. "I was born in the merciless city of New York," he began. "My father, a big time drug dealer in New York City, raised me until about age eight. I didn't really know my mother so my father was pretty much the only one that I had to look up to at the time. He was so caught up in his world of drugs, money, women, and violence that he rarely had time to teach me the values of life and how important it was to become successful. This was when I realized that it was time for me to step up and become independent.

I started smoking marijuana, selling drugs, and using them. I grew up around these things and thought that in order to survive this is what I'm going to have to do. I wanted to have all the women, cars, and money that my father had. I wanted to become the biggest and boldest drug dealer in the state, to become a "Legacy." We sat there looking at him amazed that someone could have this mentality and way of thinking as an eight year old child. "Do not think that becoming a drug dealer was an easy task. It was hard, and I had to start off with small portions before I was able make it to the top. Even though my father wasn't someone who I would say was perfect and inspirational, I still loved him."

When he was fourteen years old, Tim's father was murdered. Life became harder and he gained a colder outlook on the world. "My uncles became my keepers for some time, but they were just as bad as my father. I had no discipline from them or encouragement." Sure, he also had a grandmother "raising" him, but it wasn't the same as having a strong parental figure. We looked into his eyes and we could see a lot of emotion trapped inside of him. We may not be psychics, but we could envision this lost little boy trapped in a world of drugs and violence as he spoke to us. The only comfortable place he could turn to was the only familiar thing he knew, "the drug game". Nothing was easy from then on; he was alone in a big city.

Although the street life was grabbing a hold on him, Tim always loved school and that's where he found some comfort. There were always caring teachers that took time to help him when he was in need. But when he was making more money in a month than most people make in a year, he figured why waste his time? In the 12th grade Tim dropped out of school and continued dealing drugs.

One day while driving in the Lexus he bought at 16, Tim was pulled over and was caught with marijuana. He had an ultimatum: either have his car impounded or go to jail. Since he could pay his own bail he chose to go to jail. When he went to the court he met the young woman who would soon become his wife, but the road wasn't going to be easy.

As Tim set his sights on this young woman, he slinked over to the vending machine coolly, bought a pack of snacks, and then tried to give them to her and talk to her. Both he and the snack were rejected. He had seen her around before and he knew what kind of girl she was. She was a young lady who had respect for herself and he admired that. Tim then asked her mom if he could take her daughter out to dinner…she plainly said "No." Still, he slipped her daughter his number and two weeks later he got a call.

About seven years later, when they were married, they decided to move south to Florida. Tim gathered twenty thousand dollars and left. But in four months the money was gone, much faster than he expected. With five kids and one on the way, Tim was terrified when he received his eviction notice. He and his wife only had a few days to come up with the money. Taking the 100 dollars they had left they did the only thing they could do, go to the grocery store. You see, Tim's wife is a great cook, but besides that she is smart. With the groceries, the Misses began to cook. But when I say cook, I mean *cook*. Not the same old thing you pull out of the freezer and pop in the microwave, but traditional "soul food." Armed with the prepared food in their mini-van, the couple drove down to a local barber shop. A plan was in the works.

This is where his wife's smarts kicked in. After all, these groceries could actually make money for them. She thought about the long hours that hair stylists work and how hungry and tired they were in the shops. Together they entered the barber shop and began to talk business, bringing in a plate with them to help cajole their audience. Tim began to talk to the woman; the timing was impeccable because the empty-stomached women were just about to order some food from the restaurant next door. When asked about the food, the leader of the group asked with an attitude, "Why would we eat your food? We have no idea where it came from." Tactfully, Tim offered one plate of food to be divvied among them. If it was good they'd buy more. If not, Tim and his wife would simply be on their way.

The group of hungry women devoured the food they once questioned, and were soon longing for more. They followed the couple to the car to buy more plates. Soon the group of people turned into a small crowd as customers who initially came for a haircut and those who were potential customers of the restaurant next door ended up buying some soul food from Tim and his wife. In a period of two days they managed to sell $2,000 dollars worth of dinner plates, but to no avail. It wasn't enough to meet the amount they owed on their mortgage.

When they arrived at home all of their belongings were laid out on what they used to call their front lawn. This was by far the most embarrassing thing that ever occurred in Tim's life. While in New York he had been shot, kidnapped, and had his teeth knocked out, but the pain of this embarrassment was one he would remember for a lifetime.

A next door neighbor suggested that they go to the Salvation Army to get information on the Coalition for the Homeless. Tim took his wife, kids, their clothes, and pots of food they were preparing to sell and took his neighbors advice, leaving everything he had left with his neighbors. They went down to the Salvation Army and luckily met Ms. D, a lady that helped them transition into this unknown territory. She helped him and his family and has remained a good friend ever since.

As of now Tim has a G.E.D., a job, and is saving all the money he is making by living at the Coalition. Really, he doesn't need to be there, but he said he and his wife are dreaming of opening up a restaurant. All the money being stored away, along with the two grand, is being saved for that aspiration.

Tim is content with the life he is living and the plan he has set for himself. The place he came from is a place he wishes he had never seen, but now with a loving family by his side he has no need to look back. The only fear he has is the fear of not making it legitimately. But he believes that with the strong, smart, beautiful woman he has by his side, he can do anything.

Yeah, it's true that maybe when Tim of New York City took his first breath he had no idea what life had in store for him. However, he accepted what was handed to him and did the best he could with the hand he was dealt. Along the way he made some mistakes, but in the long run Tim showed us it doesn't matter where you are. What matters is where you are going and who you are with, and that truly everybody has a story to tell.

"What Causes Me To Be Homeless Is Bad Luck"
By Alicia Cooper and Khmoy Allen

Coalition for the Homeless. What does that mean to you, to your parents and your relatives? To everybody? *Coalition for the Homeless* means the lives of people who have gotten off track and ended up on the wrong road. It doesn't mean that they are bad people; it wasn't their fault they ended up that way. These people have lives just as we do now, but because of certain circumstances they are now at the Coalition. No one chooses to be homeless, it just happens. They need help but we shun them like they are outcasts. They want help, but we ignore them and their troubled lives. How long will these people suffer before we offer a helping hand?

As I looked at the stout old guy slouching in his chair, he looked defeated, but his eyes were determined. His name was Jackie Wilson. He was wearing a red shirt with blue jeans along with a dirty but presentable hat. Surrounding him was a mass of plastic bulky bags. As we approached him, he was asleep and we felt bad to have woken him for our interview. As we interviewed him, I was wondering why he had a cell phone, but later on I found out that he uses his cell phone to contact his sister here in Orlando, Florida. There were a lot of things that we wanted to know about him; we wanted to speak with him like friends.

He told us: "I have no struggles as an adult or with drugs and alcohol. I never was in trouble with the law. My major regret is that I never got married. I worry the most that I might die. What causes me to be homeless is bad luck."

"Nothing Worth Achieving Is Easy"
By Daphne Camille

Evelyn ("Smiley") caught our eyes in the hallway with her smile. Her presence was surprising because she was well put together and her facial expression did not show a bit of sadness. "I don't let life get me down," she told us while smiling all throughout our time together. She looked about 40 years old with short hair. Her beautiful brown face reminded us of a 10 year old. She looked strong enough to take care of herself. You could tell that she was determined to spend only a small part of her life in this place because it wasn't home to her. She had a plan that consisted of hard work and dedication in order to get a home for her and her youngest daughter.

She has had an array of bad experiences: she hasn't had a relationship with her father since the age of five, was expelled from college, sold drugs and got caught, and even had a gun pulled to her face. Out of all of this turmoil, one of her experiences brought the best out of her. "After I started smoking and realized what I was doing, I asked God to forgive me and he took the taste right out of my mouth. I haven't touched a cigarette since." Once her mind was clear and free from the worst of these experiences, she found that she still had dreams and ambitions.

Smiley was born right in our hometown, Orlando, Florida. She was the class clown in school. As a child, her dream was to become a singer. That dream of hers is still alive in her heart. Her favorite musicians are Bobby Brown, Escape, Avant, and many more. She also wanted to be a basketball star. She was a very energetic woman. Her favorite subject was science because she got a chance to dissect a frog and a snake. She enjoys cooking and woodshop.

Even though she had an unpleasant childhood watching her mother struggle to raise her eleven siblings, she has never ceased to smile; it was an eminent smile that would brighten the day of anyone.

At sixteen, Smiley had her first job at a steak house. Since then, she has had about 30 jobs; most of them include washing dishes and cooking. Her reason for having so many jobs is because of the low wages and being disrespected by her co-workers. Her relationship with her 20-year-old daughter isn't what she would want it to be. Her daughter is her motivation to keep going and to be able to provide a home for her so that she can relight the fire within.

"The circle of life thing, it happens all the time." She and her daughter had many experiences in common. They both did not have a father figure during their teenage years. They also got in trouble with the law and spent a part of their precious lives in prison. Their relationship is very rocky and it pains her to even talk about it.

Smiley became homeless when her father came back into her life thirty years later. She hasn't forgiven him for abandoning their family or for the way he has treated her mother, although her mother has accepted him with open arms and an open heart. Like her heart, her life is still in pieces and she blames him for that. She doesn't get the chance to see her mother a lot, but she makes sure that she calls her every single day because this is the only relationship she's willing to accept from her past.

As an adult, Smiley has faced several challenges. As a result, she has many regrets, mainly the way she took care of her "baby girl". Her goals are to: have a strong relationship with her daughter, forgive her father, be more motivated, rent a home, and take her mother away from her father.

Even with all of those obstacles, she is still grateful for everything that she has and hopes for. She appreciates what the Coalition is doing for her. She appreciates a warm breakfast every morning and a roof over her head. Her advice for us: "If you don't want to become homeless, you should get a job and just live."

"Dear Diary"

By Ashley Brown

Dear Diary,

How did I get here? I try to stay positive but it gets hard. Sometimes I wonder about my life and what it could have been. Don't get me wrong, I am thankful for being alive. Every morning I wake up and say the same prayer: "Lord, I thank you for allowing me to see a new day." I know that the Lord has a plan for me but what could it be. I am living my life sporadically, not knowing what I will do next. Who lives like that? I do. I cannot help but think about my life and wonder again, "How did I get here?" I look around at my roommates and see that many ask themselves that same question. When you look into their eyes, it is easy to say that "everyone has a story to tell."

 Many say that in order to know where you are going, you have to know where you came from. I hate looking back on my life because I find it unpleasant to think about. All my life I felt that I have been searching for some type of comfort. Like many families, my home was fatherless. I went through my teenage years struggling to find a replacement of comfort since he was not there. My mother was a beautiful and strong woman who raised my siblings and me with love. However, love was not the only comfort that I needed. I became a victim of peer pressure, which lead me to jail at the age of 16 for robbing a pizza parlor. At 18, I received my G.E.D. and I went looking for a job. Still searching for comfort, I started going to lots of parties and I began drinking alcohol and doing drugs at 24.

To me, drugs were my comfort. I thought I had found what I had been searching for. I started denying my family and friends and all I wanted to do was cocaine, which became my new best friend. I didn't realize that people saw that I was a drug addict because I didn't see them at all. Cocaine received all of my time and attention. To me, it was the only family that I needed. Of course, my drug addictions led me back to jail. After that, I tried about 20 different rehab centers and I eventually became homeless. I allowed cocaine to take over my life. I was penniless, depressed, and I tried to commit suicide several times. I even lost the only woman that truly loved me (besides my mother) because of this drug. That was when I finally realized that I wanted to change my life around with God.

I am now 44 years old and I have lost much of my life because of drugs. I allowed cocaine to control me for 20 years. I am now happy to say that I have been drug free for three months now because of my new relationship with God. He has allowed me to see things for the better and I pray to him everyday. He has given me many chances and this time I do not plan to throw it away.

You know what Diary? I finally found what I had been searching for all these years. It's ME. I've been struggling to find my true self, which was the only comfort that I needed. I guess you do help with people's problems. I have to go. I'll talk to you tomorrow.

Love,
Willie

"A Normal Life"
By Shardy Camargo

The first day at the shelter they arrived, the food was terrible, but they reluctantly ate it and counted their blessings. After a long day they retired to their room; the alleged clean sheets and spotless floor seemed an unknown memory. No one spoke. It was clearly and mutually understood, the children slept while they cleaned. Worn out, they rested their heads to prepare for a new day.

I anxiously walked the halls of the Coalition. Several people passed by, but I could not seem to conjure up the courage to ask for an interview. As I returned to the dining room I saw them, Luis Segarra and Elizabeth Colon. The tall, strong built Puerto Rican man held tightly to the nervous, exotic looking woman smiling with large eyes. Vending machine snacks and sodas in hand they awkwardly gazed, wondered, and smiled at the deluge of passers-by. I asked the couple if they were interested in being interviewed. They did not seem homeless to me, their nice clothes and cleanliness were not the stereotypical uniform I associated with the homeless and I hoped they would not be offended by my request.

Up close the man's face became defined, like a steamy mirror clearing up. His rugged appearance was eased by his freckles. Standing with a blank expression, he seemed stoic, or in mid-thought as he slowly moved his brown eyes across the room. His light tan skin contrasted his counter part, her exterior overpowered the room. She was beautiful and her dark luring eyes induced attention. As striking as she was, she seemed humble. They graciously agreed to speak with me and walked to the dining room.

As we spoke, Luis kept Elizabeth close, as though to protect her from something. He dominated the conversation, while she just nodded and agreed. As a native of Puerto Rico, Luis set off to New York with his mother and seven older brothers and immigrated to Brooklyn at the age of four. He knew his father but was only raised by his mother. Luis' mother was always there for him; she worked and strived to provide for the family. As a child, Luis was obedient, smart, independent, and matured fast. By the age of eight he rode the train to and from cities. As he spoke to me about his childhood, I could not help but think perhaps his father's absence influenced his current predicament. He continued telling me about his youth; "Influences affect goals in New York," he stated. "In New York you have to fight back to survive. If we lived in a better neighborhood we'd be better," he claimed. As a child he felt differently about school than everyone else. By the time he was in the fourth grade he hated school and people treated him badly. Later on, when he attended high school, he became a well-rounded student. He was well known for his talent in basketball; he was featured in many newspaper articles for his skills. When he graduated and went on to college, he grew interested in computers and majored in sociology.

Once Elizabeth began speaking she seemed a completely different person, changing from a shy exterior with minimal words to an ethnically proud Latina woman with a luminous smile. She vividly described her native land of Puerto Rico with such joy that I thought that I was in a tropical paradise. When she was two and a half years old her family emigrated from her homeland to New York. She was brought up by her mother. She knew her father but he left the family at an early stage in her life. Elizabeth remembered her mother's cooking. Like her partner's mother, she supported her family by selling food. As a child, she had aspirations of working with kids. Her dreams came true when she acquired employment in a daycare center and later in a rehabilitation center at the age of sixteen.

She described herself as a "good kid"; she never talked back to her mother and always obeyed orders. As a student of John James High School in Brooklyn, she felt it was a bad area. "My high school was very bad. Kids brought weapons to school and no one did anything about it. The teachers were afraid of the students," she explained. School just seemed like a place to go during the day and she didn't feel strongly about it. At sixteen years of age, during her junior year in high school, her mother passed away. Elizabeth lost all hope and abandoned school. After her tragic loss, she had to work in order to live; "After school, I started cleaning houses and doing anything to survive," she clarified.

When I asked the couple about marriage and their relationships, they quickly changed the topic and spoke of their two daughters; one is eight and the other is youngest five. At one point they became an extended family when they lived in Luis' sister's house. Looking back, Luis and Elizabeth felt unappreciated because Elizabeth cared for her two year old nephew who was physically incapable to walk; she loved that baby and cared for him like her own son while Luis worked. While Elizabeth and Luis worked hard, their other nephew who was an unemployed alcoholic received financial aid from his mother while they never received so much as a thank you.

Trouble began on Elizabeth's birthday. Luis' nephew picked him up with a van full of drugs. The police stopped them, suspicious about the tinted windows and found the concealed drugs. Luis said nothing and took the blame; he was later sent to jail for eight days. After the incident, they left and severed all ties with both of their remaining families. Neither of them maintain a relationship with their families. When asked why, they simply said, "because they have their own problems."

The biggest challenge they face is obtaining a home. "The worst shelters are in New York. You have to sit in a chair and fill out papers and when you are done they send you to a hotel and you have to fill out more papers when you get back; then they send you to other places," Elizabeth explained.

This couple faces many challenges and has many worries, but their biggest concerns are of their children's health. They worry they will get sick and in their environment everyone can get sick. They try to teach them to wash their hands and not touch things. Their concern for their children shows how much this couple truly cares about their children's well being.

As adults, the happiest moments in their lives have been with their children. "The only thing we have is our children," they explained to me. Receiving class pictures, good report cards, perfect attendance and love is the best part of their day. "When they give us a hug and tell us how much they love us it just brightens our day; I mean, we're depressed because we have to live here but our kids are happy and that just makes things easier," Luis explained.

They left me briefly to pick up their children from the daycare. As they walked back in the dining room, I was touched with the sight of them as a family. Despite all the things they went through, they held a positive attitude and the two girls seemed as content as they could be. The eldest had a radiant smile that could be seen across the room; she held close to her little sister and pulled her curly hair into a tight ponytail as we spoke. They sat together as tight as they could, it was a very happy sight. I almost cried, but I didn't want to make them uncomfortable. I collected myself and continued the interview.

Their introspection was surprising. Luis regretted not continuing basketball but he stated that if he continued he might not have his family today. Elizabeth wished she would have finished school, as horrible as it was, but would not take anything back; "I have no regrets, just being here and not having a chance to have a job is something I wish I could change," she stated.

Luis explained his daily routine; everyday he drops off his daughters at school, goes to work, picks them up, helps with homework, and eats. "The food isn't good, the place isn't clean, but after a while you get hungry and the food tastes better," he stated. Indeed hunger is the best spice, something you hate could become tasty after a long time without eating, and in such harsh conditions one has to adjust and make do with what they have. Elizabeth and Luis told me what their dream life would be: a house, two cars, a dog, and a normal day to day routine. Most people would consider this boring. In our modern society, people want to do new and audacious things, where this family wants what most take for granted, a "normal" life. "People say they got it bad, but they got it better. We got it worse." Luis said. From all the things this family has gone through, they serve as an example of how hard life could be when homeless.

    The interview was over; I could not believe it ended so soon. The whole family sat patiently smiling, seeming as though expecting another question. No words came to mind and I felt like I should say something encouraging. But they have heard it all, big words and recycled phrases. All I could say was "thank you" as I got up and looked in each of their eyes one more time. We parted ways, I did not look back, and I felt nothing. When I stepped onto the bus it seemed as though nothing had changed. I was wrong; I had no idea how soon my emotions would hit me and how

dramatically this experience would change me…

*The Coalition for the Homeless would like to clarify their food is cooked with love by the volunteers in the community who care about our clients. All meals are well balanced, adhering to federal nutritional guidelines. As for the cleanliness of the facility, it is home to 240 people, half of whom are children. Messes are being created constantly. There is no cleaning staff; residents are responsible for keeping it clean. We wash all sheets before issuing them to clients. Our sheets are donated, so they are often stained, but they are washed.

Reflections

Britney Bernard

Before going into the Homeless shelter and meeting Edward, I was kind of nervous because I did not know what to expect or what his reaction would be; but as the interview progressed, I started to relax and feel comfortable with him. He was compassionate and very nice. He was also very open with me. After meeting and talking with him I felt a lot better about myself and what I've done. I left the shelter that day feeling as though I had brought a touch of sunshine to Edwards life. I will always remember Edward and how nice and polite he was to me.

Thien C. Pham

Before visiting the homeless shelter, a feeling of nervousness and uncertainty hit me. I did not have much courage in myself because I have never really socialized with homeless people. My feelings started to change after I met Miguel. His willingness to talk made me feel comfortable and more compassionate. After the visit to the Coalition I felt proud because I finally did something I thought I couldn't do.

Candice Haughton

Before I arrived at the Coalition, I never knew that the world could be so cold. I wasn't only ignorant but also ungrateful. The clothes on my back, the bed I sleep in, and simply having my state of mind wasn't something I was thankful for. I was blinded by my own life and unconscious of the troubles of others.

At the Coalition, I felt like a child, a small child being force-fed the realities of the world; it was overwhelming. My eyes were opened and I was somewhat overwhelmed with emotion. Now that I am aware of what life really is, I thank God every day for simply living and having a place to call my own.

<u>Duan Zirkle</u>

Meeting with Smiley was a great experience for me. It made me look at life from a new point of view. People lose things while others gain, and nothing in life is written on stone tablets. Life can be difficult when one loses but to have the courage to face your problems is respectable. To have a positive outlook on life during these times like Smiley is even more admirable.

<u>Calvin Hitnarain</u>

Before I went to the coalition I didn't really care about people who I didn't know. I usually ignored them and just walked by when I saw someone asking for money. When I went to the Coalition I was surprised to see what other people went through, yet they were no different from you or me. I saw young children like me living there with hardly anything to hold onto. Now when I see people asking for money I don't just walk by. I take a look at the person to see how that person is and if he/she really needs the money. I now realize just how unfortunate some people are.

Alicia Cooper

I felt really cautious but excited to be at the Coalition. The atmosphere seemed similar to my old neighborhood and there were homeless people everywhere. The hours rapidly passed as Khmoy and I interviewed our friend Jackie. The homeless are okay and are people just like us. I feel comfortable and carefree around them now. I enjoyed myself.

Jessica Laracuente

Before going to the shelter I found myself a bit nervous about the whole thing. I had never been to a homeless shelter and I didn't know what to expect. When we arrived I found myself speechless. Never in my life have I ever seen so many people in need. As we walked around and began speaking, my heart went out to each and every one of them. The more they told me, the more I became interested and wanted to hear their stories. I walked away from this shelter as a changed person. Viewing homeless people and life differently, I now have a greater appreciation for life and the things I have.

Bionca Bachelor

Before I entered the Coalition I was thinking, "I don't want to be here." But as I began my interview my state of mind began to change. The person I interviewed made me feel as if we had everything in common because she encountered the same life struggles as I am experiencing now. After I left I did not view my interviewee as a homeless person, but as one of my friends. Visiting the homeless shelter really helped me to see that everyone is human and we should be ONE.

Tiffany Longjohn

When I was first approached about this opportunity I was a little scared. In my mind I thought, "How are we supposed to ask these people about their personal lives?" I thought it was going to be a hard situation. After coming in and talking to Mr. Frank Crosby, I left the homeless shelter feeling like a better person.

Sympson Placide

Before having the opportunity to visit the homeless shelter, my frame of mind was completely different than it is now. I thought the homeless individuals were thoughtless and guilty of their circumstances. After that visit I learned that not everyone wanted to be in that situation, it is just destiny and the path they chose at an early age.

Thien An Pham

Before I interviewed Damien, I thought homeless people totally gave up their own dignity and respect to be isolated from the world. However, when I had the opportunity to actually talk to a young homeless person like Damien, I could see in his eyes that he was excited that there were still people that care about him. After the interview I knew that his family members abandoned him at an early age; I realized that he lacks the love and compassion in his life that most people receive from their families. I did learn something about him because he didn't give up.

Almendra Vegas

You know that feeling of confidence where a person believes they can do anything? I had the complete opposite feeling while on the bus going towards the homeless shelter. I was a nervous wreck! Butterflies were in my stomach when we arrived. But I soon I became comfortable. It turned out to be a great experience.

Serenitye Massey

When my partner and I walked up to Frank, we both really didn't know what to expect. Emotions crept over us….What were we going to say? Would he like us? How could we reach out to him? But when we introduced ourselves to him, he was more than friendly. He was unlike anyone we have ever met. We shared stories, asked questions and got to know the real Frank D. Crosby. He is someone we will never forget and the experience that helped build our characters.

Shaneetra Chappell

While I entered the shelter, I was astonished at how many people were laying down, sleeping on the cement. Children were running around in broken glass with no shoes. I felt bad, like I was teasing them as I walked down the street in my $50.00 shoes, expensive jewelry, and everything in my purse. When I saw a couple of good-looking dressed men in the corner, I approached them. I found it coincidental that both men's names were Tim.

As Tim told me about his life, I looked into his eyes. I saw a hardworking man, but how could this man be here? How could he bare this type of situation? Maybe it was his way of living. I realized that I was showing the bias I promised myself not to show. Maybe he liked it here, maybe the shelter was good for him. It may have seemed sad to me, but it could be a good thing for him.

I left that Coalition with optimism, much different than the nervous, ashamed, and frightened feeling that I entered the coalition with. I realized that the people at the Coalition were probably there because they were using it as a stepping stone towards success. I realized this was not the same for all of them, but it was the feeling I left with. It changed me.

Daphne Camille

I was very uncomfortable when I found out that I was going to a homeless shelter. When I got there and saw how they were living, I felt sorry for these people. However, after talking to them, I found out that some of them were better off than some other people I knew. I would go back anytime. They don't choose to be homeless, but they wake up every day trying and hoping to get a better life.

Kimonia Levy

Before I arrived at the homeless shelter I didn't even care about the homeless. I felt as if they deserved to be in that predicament. While I was there my feelings changed, and as I listened to their story, I felt extremely sorry for them because I realized that no one chooses to be homeless. When I left I was so sad! The person who I interviewed looked as if he knew he didn't belong there.

Ray Khan

It started out as a normal day, like every other Saturday, but it wasn't. That day the Beta Club was going to the homeless shelter. I was anxious and nervous but my feelings were justified; they were homeless! When I got there, it was completely different than what I had imagined. These people were nice and they looked fairly happy. My feelings about them changed from fearful to comfortable. They were good at heart.

Moise Civil

Initially, I thought homeless people were people without dreams. I thought they were incapable and inadequate. While spending time at the Coalition, the woman I spoke with made me realize that they are somebody. They have dreams and some of them are working very hard towards those dreams. After I left, I understood homelessness could happen to anybody.

Jose Vasquez

Before I went to the Coalition for the Homeless, I was kind of nervous. I was nervous because I had never been to a homeless shelter before in my life. But when I got there I was so relaxed that when we left I wanted to go back in again. I enjoyed talking to them. They were respectful and courteous people.

Khmoy Allen

Before I went to the homeless shelter, I didn't know what to expect. It was like I was going to visit a foreign country. I had never been there before and it was a completely different scene than what I was used to. I was surprised when I realized that the living conditions were better than I had thought. Living on the streets was worse. When I left, I felt thankful for the experience and I thanked Ms. Bohn for giving me the opportunity to see that there was more happening in my community than what I usually paid attention to.

Stephanie Cineas

I will be the first to admit, before I went to the homeless shelter, I thought that homeless people brought their situation upon themselves. I believed that if they wanted to fix their lives, they would have done it. When a homeless person would ask me for change, the first thing that came to my mind was that he or she was going to waste my money. Every time I saw one of them holding a sign, I thought it was just a scam. I thought I was superior, but I was wrong. Homeless people are *people*. After speaking to Damien, my eyes were opened.

Tuyen Pham

Visiting the homeless shelter was a really new experience for me. I had never set foot in a homeless shelter before. I went anyway because I wanted to understand more about homeless life. I interviewed Victor. At first I thought he was mean, but the more I talked to him, the more I realized that he was actually a kind, open, and interesting person. After talking to Victor, I became conscious of how much these people had been through. They have helped me appreciate my life and I have a completely different opinion of them now. I'm glad I went because the experience has taught me that one cannot judge a book by its cover. Everyone is the same; no one is less or more important than another.

Vina Nguyen

Before I went to the homeless shelter, I thought that the people in there were very poor and that all they did was drink beer and stay angry. But when I got there, I saw the situation differently because most of them were living with their family. They had a place to live and food to eat. However, I still feel sorry for them because they haven't had much luck in their lives. The person we interviewed,

Victor, was very nice and he answered all of our questions. I felt so bad for him! He advised us to do things the right way, to stay in school and be a good student.

Kerline Delva

Having to wake up every morning not by someone you love, not in something you call home is really hard. When I arrived at the homeless shelter for the first time it was really hard for me. Walking in changed my whole perspective on homeless people. Some don't have a choice because of their numerous struggles. Today I have nothing but respect for them and their accomplishments.

Natacha Daverman

Before I went to the homeless shelter I already knew what to expect. I knew that people were going to be walking around, talking, or playing cards. What I didn't know was *who* they were. I also didn't know how they were going to react to the questions we were going to ask them. After my interview, I came to the conclusion that they actually wanted to share their life stories with us and now, I have nothing but respect for them.

Malaika Joseph

The first thought that came to my mind when I first entered the homeless shelter was that these people were not living well. After talking with one of them, I realized how simple their life was. I didn't look down on them because of their lifestyles. Instead, I appreciated talking to them. In a way, these people were just like me. The only reason I wasn't living like them was because of the God's grace. Helping them really changed the way I used to think of them. I remember how I used to judge them according to anything they did. Now, I respect them and I vow to support them as much as I can.

Vincent Pham

I felt uncomfortable at the thought of visiting the homeless shelter because it was an unfamiliar place to me. Since it was full of poor people, I assumed it was a dirty place until I went there myself. I came to think of it as a decent dwelling whose inhabitants changed my whole life. I now have a different outlook on life, especially when it comes to homeless people and the way they act. They have gained my respect.

Peter Joseph

I used to be scared of showing the homeless people what I thought of them. If I was walking down the streets and a homeless person walked past me and asked me how I was doing, I would just ignore him. My opinion was that he didn't care, he was just talking nonsense. But after having a forty- five minute conversation with a homeless person, I learned more about what they went through and knowing that they are still going through it has changed me. Now when I see one of them, I don't wait for them to talk to me. Instead, I walk up to them and ask them about their day.

Fabienne Elie

My first visit to the homeless shelter was nerve-racking. I'm not the kind of person who walks up to new people and starts talking to them willingly. I usually wait for them to make the first step. So when I learned that we were going to ask people to tell us about their lives, I was worried because I knew there was a big chance they might reject us. Talking to Luis, Elizabeth, and John didn't change my whole life but it did change my perspective on the world. All the things I whine about were nothing compared to what they were going through. When I left, I knew that I was going home and there would be food waiting for me and when I felt like it, I was going to sink into my warm, soft bed and sleep without worries. Unlike them, I wasn't concerned about essential things like food.

After visiting the homeless shelter, I stopped thinking of homeless people as individuals who deserved to be homeless. I had sympathy for the children but when it came to the adults, I used to think that if they wanted to change their lives, they would have done so already. I had never once stopped to think about how they had become homeless or why they were still homeless. But now I do. Ever since I talked to three people who managed to smile and laugh even if they were living in a homeless shelter, I've had a new found respect for them. To me, these people are some of the most courageous people on Earth. They have helped me appreciate my life and through my experience, I have learned not to take anything for granted; food, money, even happiness. I'm very glad I went to the homeless shelter that Saturday and even if I had to risk rejection, I would do it all over again.

Alicia Greene

Weeks before preparing for the homeless shelter, I was very excited but nervous at the same time. As the date approached, I was even more excited to learn about the way and lives of people whom I did not know and was not accustomed to. When I got there, I was introduced to an environment that I had never even taken a second look at. I saw that homeless people were people, not just label bearers. They were living a life they had not chosen. The ones I met *were not looking for coins, but for change.* They wanted to belong somewhere. Now I have a totally different but better outlook on life. I am more grateful and aware of everything.

Shardy Camargo

During one BETA Club delegate meeting, Ms. Bohn announced that she chose us to be the group that will participate on an idea she had. She wanted us interview the homeless in the Coalition we had been to and write about their life stories. I was so excited to be a part of something so influential but frightened at the same time because the only time I had gone to the Coalition I had watched a movie with only the children. I did not know what to expect from the adults and was unsure if I could handle interviewing someone on such a sensitive subject. Despite my worries, I entered the Coalition with confidence although it took me a while to build up the courage to ask someone. I was graced by the presence of two charming people, Luis Segarra and Elizabeth Colon. The interview went by smoothly and I was glad that they shared their personal stories with me. After collecting all the information, I attended writing workshops along with the other BETA delegates, one being in the University of Florida. I was surprised how many good people there are in this world, the University of Florida had supported our book and message by supplying us with accommodations, breakfast, lunch, and dinner, and several rooms and computers to work with on their campus. It was a lovely workshop that really made me think of what I was doing and how I should learn from my experience and help others as well.

All my life I had felt no sympathy towards the homeless, as if they were some bad lazy people who had to get their act together and take action. When I thought of a homeless person I only thought of a dirty, stinky, old hobo. My complacency and ignorance was my downfall, it had made my heart cold and full of callus, and my stereotypical thoughts had made me impervious to empathy. Through my whole experience I have learned that everyone is affected by others and some people have extremely limited control over their lives; people obviously do not choose to be homeless, and in most cases it is very difficult to get by in this world because not everyone has the same opportunities as others. Although it is an almost instinctual habit, I have learned not to judge people. I also try not to let anything go to waste, whether it is food or a happy moment, value what you have, keep it, and store it safe away. Through the stories people have shared with me I learned to value my life no matter what happens because there are millions of people who have lives far worse than I do but somehow they find a way to smile. I have found these are not just stories, they are real life.